The Homeowner's Guide to Contracting, Building, and Remodeling

Save a Fortune by Learning What Contractors Don't Want You to Know

The Homeowner's Guide to Contracting, Building, and Remodeling

Save a Fortune by Learning What Contractors Don't Want
You to Know

by Joe Oswald

Contents

Figure 1. The 1920s-era Spanish Revival home with stone turret where I was born and where I continue to raise my own family. My parents purchased this home in 1968. I moved back with my family in 2015. We spent three years renovating the inside before we tackled the three-level addition on the rear of the home that replaced a garage that was falling down with a new garage, new basement, new kitchen, and new master bedroom suite.

Dedication

This book is dedicated to my parents, who raised me in a beautiful, historic home in a wonderful historic neighborhood on the south side of Chicago. This home inspired my love of architecture, preservation, and renovation.

Acknowledgments

I would like to thank all the people who made our home renovation project possible, especially Joe Carroll, Allan Boerner, Pat McGrath, and Luke Sekula. Your efforts and skill made the project possible. I would also like to thank all our neighbors, who endured the mess, the noise, and the dumpsters during the initial renovation process, then again through the building of the addition. I would especially like to thank our neighbors Tom and Liz, who bore the brunt of the construction process, and for allowing us to move forward with our plans.

Certificate of Achievement

Presented this Eleventh day of May, 2004

Joseph C. Oswald

In recognition of the successful completion of:

GENERAL CONTRACTING

Certificate of Completion
Moraine Valley Community College

Robert J. O'Brien—Instructor

R J O'BRIEN & ASSOCIATES
7601 SOUTH KOSTNER, SUITE 202
CHICAGO, ILLINOIS 60652

About the Author

Joe Oswald was born and raised in Chicago's historic Beverly Hills neighborhood, where he continues to live and raise his own family. When he was twenty-one years old, he passed the Illinois real estate exam and began selling real estate with a local Century 21 office. He also worked as a new home consultant for a real estate developer and took a general contracting class to learn the ins and outs of home building. Joe put this knowledge to use when he renovated a vintage 1929 Chicago bungalow, doing much of the work himself, and recently when he acted as his own general contractor in putting a three-level addition onto his 1929 Spanish Revival home.

Additionally, Joe has a master's degree in history from DePaul University and a master's degree in educational administration. He has worked as a Chicago public high school history teacher for over twenty years, served as chairman of the history department and on the school leadership team for nine years. He continues to teach Chicago history and an AP research course.

His other books include *Chicago's Beverly/Morgan Park Neighborhood*, a book about the historic Beverly Hills and Morgan Park communities published by Arcadia Publishing as part of their Images of America series. Joe has also written a vocabulary improvement book titled *Vocabulary for Champions* and continues to give presentations about the neighborhood to various community groups.

For more information, please visit his website at www.joeoswald.com or email Joe at joe@joeoswald.com.

Figure 2. The living room of our Spanish Revival home is accented by a cathedral ceiling with stained beams, plaster walls with a Spanish stucco design, iron gates and railings, arched French doors, a fireplace, and wall sconces. A 1960s-era parquet floor was pulled up, revealing the home's original oak floors.

Introduction

To live a fulfilled life, we need to keep creating the "what is next" of our lives. Without dreams and goals there is no living, only merely existing, and that is not why we are here.
—Mark Twain

For many people, building a new home is a once-in-a-lifetime opportunity and a chance to construct a home exactly the way they want it from the ground up. Other people choose to remodel or expand their home with an addition. Other people will not even consider buying a home that needs work or any amount of updating. Many home buyers today want an updated, modern-looking home that is move-in ready. Some people are put off by the perceived hassles or cost of remodeling or cannot see past the way a home looks when they first see it and cannot visualize the possibilities of what it could be like once remodeled.

Building or renovating a home can, indeed, be one of the most time-consuming and expensive projects in a person's life, but it can also be one of the most rewarding and long-lasting endeavors anyone undertakes. Some homeowners relish the opportunity to remodel a home or tackle an addition because it gives them the opportunity to create a space that is exactly the way they want and prefer to remodel and expand rather than moving. Other people have ties to their community and love their home and wish to update it rather than look for another house. Buying a home that needs work is also a great way to get a good price and reap greater rewards of appreciation once the home is remodeled. For these people, the benefits of remodeling outweigh some of the hassles, and they can enjoy the fruits of their effort for the rest of their lives.

With dozens of photographs that detail the construction process from beginning to end, this book is meant to help you with that process. This book is not about how to build a house; it is about learning how to save money when building a home or addition by showing you how to control your costs whether you work with a general contractor or act as your own, as I did. We saved between $50,000 to $100,00 over the estimates of general contractors I received bids from before deciding to tackle the project myself, mostly by avoiding their markups and being able to choose my own materials and subcontractors. The builder markups are the extra fees general contractors tack onto each aspect of a project above what their subcontractors charge them. It is extra profit built into their estimates that the homeowner never sees. The builder markup is the secret of general contractors and builders. Learn how to avoid their markups, and you can save a fortune. This book will show you how to avoid builder markups while covering some of the important aspects of building a home or an addition.

While not without headaches, acting as my own general contractor was truly one of the best decisions I ever made and one of the most rewarding experiences of my life. While this book focuses more on renovating and adding on to an existing home, the information in this book applies just as much to building a home from the ground up and will help you whether you go the owner-builder route as I did or hire a general contractor.

The reasons I wrote this book include the fact I could not believe how much of a markup most general contractors factor into their estimates when bidding on a project. After doing my own research before committing to our addition and with all the previous experience I had in selling real estate, working for a home builder, and renovating our first home, I knew some of the estimates we got were flawed and inflated and, in some cases, made no sense. I figured this addition was going to be the biggest and most expensive investment of my life, so I spent a great deal of time planning and researching how it would be built and how much it might cost before even talking to any contractors. I talked to a couple of well-known and established general contractors who, no doubt, would have been fine to work with and would have done a great job, but the prices were so exorbitant we never could have afforded the addition. These were contractors who were used to building high-end homes in some of Chicago's exclusive suburbs and had beautiful showrooms, project managers, their own architects, and impressive credentials. They were professional and very knowledgeable, but they also wanted to charge the same rates for their work on the south side of Chicago where I lived as they did in exclusive suburbs with multimillion-dollar homes, such as Hinsdale and Oakbrook. Even if we could have afforded their prices, it was not worth it for our addition. Money aside, the cost was not justified given the real estate market even in the upper-middle-class neighborhood where we lived. Resale value and a market appraisal for a home equity or construction loan to pay for the addition might have been problematic. I did not want to risk putting more money into the house than it might be worth after the addition was completed. I am sure these contractors would have done a fine job, but I also would have paid over $100,000 more than I wound up paying by acting as my own general contractor.

When we finally got bids from other, smaller local contractors, I was less than impressed. For example, we wanted a new basement under the new kitchen that would connect to our existing basement. The estimates for a new, unfinished basement ranged from $2,500 from one contractor to $25,000 from another. I knew the $25,000 was really high, given the size of the new basement, but I also knew $2,500 was ridiculous because you cannot even have all the excavated dirt hauled away for $2,500, let alone do all the excavating and pour the foundation. One contractor left the cost of lumber and other materials off his initial rough framing estimate! One contractor's estimate for plumbing was $27,000 while two other estimates came in at under $10,000. I even had one contractor quote me a price of $9,000 to replicate four interior wood doors that would match the common 1920s-era single-panel doors in the existing house. I thought that price seemed high, and that was just for four inside doors. I wound up finding several matching doors in good shape at a salvage business for under $1,000.

The numbers were all over the place and did not add up. There was no way I could accurately predict my final cost based on these estimates, knowing there were already so many mistakes and discrepancies among the bids. There was also no way I could be confident that a construction loan would be approved with these estimates. I even had one contractor tell me the city would never approve my permit to rebuild the garage as living space in the same footprint because it was on the rear lot line. He wanted to build the addition on the side of the house instead. This would have negated all the reasons for wanting the addition on the rear of the home in the first place and destroyed our back and side yards while completely ruining the look of the house. My initial instinct was that this contractor was trying to get me to commit to something he could build right away rather than waiting out a possibly more involved or lengthy permitting process, even if it meant building me an addition I did not want.

I decided to find out for myself and took a trip down to the city's zoning department with the survey of the house and lot. Sure enough, my gut instinct was correct. There was nothing uncommon about what I was asking to do, but it would, indeed, require a slight zoning adjustment and approval, which would take extra time and extra money beyond a standard building permit. It would be well worth the extra time and money to have the addition the way I wanted it and the way that made sense (more about this process in the Chapter 2). Either that contractor did not know what he was talking about, or he knew full well and just wanted a project he could start right away. It was after all this hassle dealing with these contractors that I decided to go it alone and act as my own general contractor, and it was one of the best decisions I ever made. I still wound up saving $50,000 on the bids I received from these smaller contractors and had complete control over the planning and budgetary aspects of the project.

I also decided to write this book because I learned so much during this process, and I wanted to share that knowledge. I spent countless hours researching products, methods, and materials that went into our home that are unfamiliar to many people. I want others to benefit from this knowledge without having to start from scratch and spend countless hours reading home improvement magazines, websites, and books as I did. Many of these products and methods are not covered in other home improvement or remodeling books, and a lot of contractors and subcontractors were not familiar with some of the things I wanted. For example, I decided I wanted hot water (hydronic) radiant floor heat in the addition, but some general contractors and even some heating, ventilation, and air conditioning (HVAC) contractors did not know how to install this type of system, even though these systems are featured on home remodeling shows such as *This Old House* all the time. Small-duct high-velocity air-conditioning systems have been around for decades, are a staple in historic home renovations, and have been featured on *This Old House* many times as well. My parents even had this type of system installed in the house decades ago, but these systems are not even mentioned in some of the best-selling contracting and remodeling books that I have read. Many HVAC contractors do not know how to install these units because they are only used to working with conventional central air-conditioning and heating systems.

There are many examples like this covered in this book. This, along with my love of writing and passion for renovating, led me to write this book and share my experiences, my knowledge, and dozens of photographs of a real construction project in a way that is meant to be straightforward, easy to follow, and, most of all, practical. Like I told myself, it's my house and my money, so I should play the biggest role in the construction project by educating myself about as many aspects of construction and contracting as possible. It certainly paid off, and I am sure it will for the reader as well.

What This Book Covers

This book covers the ins and outs of building an addition and remodeling a home from the perspective of the homeowner. This book can serve as an invaluable and practical guide for your project, whether you are working with a general contractor or acting as your own and hiring all the subcontractors who do the actual work. It covers the major aspects of building, including financing the project, working with an architect, obtaining permits, finding and hiring subcontractors, getting estimates (called bids), working with inspectors, excavation, foundations, rough framing, plumbing, electrical, roofing, heating and air-conditioning systems, insulation, kitchens and baths, and many other features that go into a home. I tried to cite specific sources of information whenever possible. The Kindle version of this book has active hyperlinks in the bibliography to many of the articles I cite, hyperlinks to videos, and full color photographs not found in the paperback edition. I found the inspirational quotes at the beginning of each chapter in an article in *Entrepreneur* magazine (Zipkin 2017).

Objectives of This Book

- Show how to avoid builder markups when building or remodeling;
- Show more about the contracting and building process;
- Show how to plan and finance your project;
- Show how to complete a project on time and within budget;
- Show how to control costs and avoid setbacks;
- Show how to obtain estimates on materials and labor;
- Show how to find and hire subcontractors;
- Show how to apply for permits and work with inspectors; and
- Show the practical uses and installation methods of many home improvement products.

This book is not about the technical aspects of house construction but about how to plan and oversee the construction by hiring all the subcontractors yourself instead of paying a general contractor a fortune to do the same thing. There are some excellent books that cover every aspect of the building process. These books are often filled with a lot more information than the typical homeowner needs to know, especially for most remodeling projects, but they are a great resource. These books have a wealth of great technical information but sometimes leave out many of the more practical things homeowners need to know when remodeling. One book I read when I took my general contracting class is *How to Build, Plan, Contract, and Build Your Own Home* by Richard M. Scutella and Dave Herbele. Another great book is *The Complete Guide to Contracting Your Home* by Kent Lester and Dave McGuerty. The first book is basically an encyclopedia of the building process and has a lot of good information related to how homes are actually built. The second book covers much of the same but also contains a lot of information on planning and inspections. If you are like me and want to know everything you can about a project before pursing it, these are great books, but they do not go into a lot of detail on working as your own general contractor. Still, I recommend reading as many books and articles about the various aspects of construction and remodeling as possible.

This book takes a lot of the information and condenses it into what I consider the most important and practical things a homeowner should know and consider when building a home or planning a renovation or addition. This book covers the main ins and outs of the construction and remodeling process for the homeowner, with an emphasis on what to include and how to save money by controlling your costs. Knowing the true cost of the work that is to be performed, rather than just relying on the prices quoted by general contractors, is the key to saving money. Contractor bids often include their stated profits (their fee for the job) but not the hidden extra profits that are tucked into their markups. Knowing the true cost of the materials and labor needed to perform a certain task is the single most important aspect of controlling the costs associated with a construction project and invaluable when negotiating prices with general contractors and subcontractors.

Acting as Your Own General Contractor

If you are building a new home from scratch in a new subdivision, chances are a builder or general contractor is the one selling the lots and building the homes. Other subdivisions are laid out by land developers who sell the lots to contractors or directly to home buyers, who then find their own general contractors to build the home. If you are renovating or adding on to an existing home, there are many options available, depending on the scope of the work. Renovating a home might or might not require an architect or permits; it depends on the scope of the work and the local building codes.

Some people are very handy or in the trades themselves, so doing a lot of the remodeling work themselves is not a problem. Most homeowners are not in this situation, however. When it comes to a major remodel or an addition, most people look for a licensed contractor to do the work, just as they do when building a home from the ground up. There are many valid reasons for this, including the fact that most homeowners do not know much about construction and remodeling, do not want to deal with the day-to-day aspects of a large undertaking, and do not have the time or the patience for such projects. The thought of applying for permits, working with architects and subcontractors, planning and designing a project, and choosing the proper materials and methods is daunting. For most people, this all might seem overwhelming, and many homeowners have no idea where to start, so they call a general contractor. Even if you hire a general contractor, the information in this book can help you decide on a plan that is best for you and still save you a great deal of time and money.

That being said, when possible, acting as your own general contractor is the single best way to save a fortune when building, remodeling, or expanding a home. General contractors make their money by hiring all the subcontractors who do the actual work and by overseeing the entire project. General contractors charge a fee for their services but also usually tack on more money, or markups, to the work done by each subcontractor, thereby increasing the profits over their stated fees. For example, a general contractor might get a quote from an HVAC contractor for materials and labor to install the heating and air-conditioning system in an addition. The quote might come in at $10,000, but the contractor might state in the overall bid for the project that the HVAC cost is $15,000. The difference in price is the builder's markup, and the homeowner will never know the difference because subcontractors never reveal their prices to the homeowner. They protect their relationships with the general contractors, who often give them a lot of work. They also understand that this is how the industry functions. Think of it as wholesale versus retail price. The cost for the subcontractor to do the job is the wholesale price. The price the general contractor turns around and charges the homeowner is the retail price. The difference is the builder markup. The problem for the homeowner is the fact that there are numerous goods and services that go into building a home, and if the general contractor marks up a lot of those items, it can add up to fortune by the time a home or addition is built.

In fact, before we started our addition, I called an HVAC company to request an estimate. When I told them the address, they said they had already provided an estimate for our work. I did not know it at first but soon realized this was a company one of the general contractors I got a bid from used. I explained to them that I was not using that contractor, but they still would not give me an estimate because they didn't want me to know the difference between their cost and what the builder might have already told me, thereby protecting their relationship with the general contractor. Needless to say, I never used that HVAC company.

By acting as your own contractor, you are eliminating the middleman and thereby eliminating the substantial fees and hidden markups general contractors charge, which could easily save you tens of thousands of dollars on a large project. The savings can be put back into the home to include things you otherwise might not be able to afford. How much you can save by acting as your own contractor rather than hiring a general contractor depends on many factors. Experts peg the savings at 20 percent or more of the total cost of the project just by eliminating the builder markup (Lester and McGuerty 2016, 10). That amounts to a $100,000 savings on $500,000 new home and a $40,000 savings on a $200,000 addition. When combined with the ability to seek your own competitive bids and choose your materials, the savings can far surpass just the 20 percent builder markup. Again, this depends on many factors, such as the scope of the work, the builder, the current market conditions, the materials used, and the amount of the fees and markups included in a contractor's bid. Keep in mind that you do not see the markups in a bid, and often, a builder is getting a contractor's discount on materials and other items from their suppliers but still charges the homeowner the full retail price. Like it or not, it is just the way the industry functions.

Before I decided to act as my own general contractor, I met with and received bids from a few contractors, each of whom I asked to break down their estimates in a line item fashion for each aspect of the job: rough framing, trim work, plumbing, electrical, heating and air conditioning, insulation, concrete and masonry, et cetera. Each bid also listed the contractor's fee as overhead and profit. In the various bids I received, each contractor charged a fee of about $30,000. This would be the money they would make from doing all the work. However, tucked into each line item were additional markups I would never have been aware of without getting my own estimates and doing my own research.

I found thousands and thousands of dollars of padded costs built into their estimates.

Often, the estimates general contractors receive from their subcontractors vary, and that can affect their overall estimate to the homeowner, but some of the prices I was given for some aspects of the job really made me wonder. I was turned off enough to know I didn't want to work with them. I would have preferred they just give me the true-to-cost estimates and increase the amount of the stated profit/fee if they wanted more money for the job rather than trying to hide additional costs through their hidden markups. One bid I received listed the painting cost as $11,000, when I actually got the entire addition painted by a great painting crew I had used before for less than $4,500. One contractor's bid for central heating and air conditioning was over $15,000, when the quote I got from an HVAC contractor was $9,500. (I put the estimated savings toward installing radiant floor heating instead of a forced-air system.) Insulation bids from the contractors raged from a few thousand dollars to over $11,000, and some did not even specify what type of insulation would be used. I had a reputable insulation company blow in cellulose insulation and fire caulk the entire addition for just over $4,000. The quote I got from one contractor for four matching interior wood doors for $9,000 was blown away when I purchased eight identical doors in good shape from a salvage company for $750, which included delivery. The list goes on and on. You can see how just avoiding the builder markups can save a fortune.

Item	Contractor Price	My Price	Savings
HVAC	$14,800	$9,800	$5,000
Insulation	$11,195	$4,095	$7,100
Painting	$10,705	$4,150	$6,555

Total Savings: $18,655

As you can see, I saved a fortune on just these three items by getting my own estimates and hiring my own people. The feeling that I was being taken advantage of was a major turnoff and made me question how many other things the contractors were not telling me. It also made me worry about other costs not already included that might arise later, possibly blowing my budget and jeopardizing the entire project. The lack of transparency cost the contractors the job. Rather than paying what I thought were inflated prices, I decided to act as my own contractor to save money and put the savings back into the home by including items I otherwise might not have considered.

I know you might be thinking that acting as your own general contractor is something you could or would never do, even if it meant saving a fortune. You might think you do not have the knowledge or background, or there is no way you would have the time to undertake such a project. But it is possible. Even if you decide to hire a project manager to oversee things while you are working your day job, you could still wind up saving an enormous amount of money. In fact, retired tradesmen are often the perfect candidates to hire as project managers, and some general contractors are even open to the idea of cutting their fees if the homeowner plays a bigger role in the project. Some contractors will also let homeowner use their own subcontractors.

However you decide to pursue your project, there are three things to keep in mind:

1. The principles in this book can still save you a great deal of money, even if you hire a general contractor.
2. Being open to the idea of being your own contractor does not mean you have to do any of the physical work yourself.
3. You do not have to be an expert in all aspects of construction and remodeling to act as your own contractor.

General contractors don't do the work themselves; they farm the work out to others and charge a fee for their services. It is the subcontractors who need to have the knowledge and skills to do their specific jobs properly. The general contractor simply acts like a conductor in an orchestra, making sure all parties do their jobs in a proper and timely manner. General contractors simply line up and hire all the subcontractors to perform the individual jobs in building a home. Contractors already know and have relationships with the subcontractors they use. The hardest part of this endeavor for the homeowner is finding the right subcontractors to do the work.

In some states, general contractors are required to pass a written test proving they understand the basic principles of building and construction. However, in many states, such as Illinois, general contractors are not required to pass a test to obtain their contracting license. It is the various subcontractors who have to prove certain competencies to acquire and maintain their licenses. General contractors have to be licensed if they are building homes for other people, but homeowners generally do not have to meet any special requirements to oversee their own projects. However, some of the work will need to be performed by licensed subcontractors, such as a licensed electrician or concrete and masonry contractor. In Chicago, acting as your own contractor is known as self-certifying, and it is a relatively simple permitting process that your architect will most likely be able to guide you through. Any extra money you pay your architect for his time will be well worth it compared to what you would pay a general contractor. Before you decide on this route, however, check with your local municipality to learn the rules and requirements for self-certifying to see if this is an option.

As the homeowner, if you are organized, detailed oriented, have a solid plan, know what you want, are firm and fair, and are willing do to some legwork and put in some time and effort, you will be able to control every aspect of your project. You can also save a fortune at the same time simply by hiring and coordinating all the subcontractors yourself. It is not without an investment of time and effort, but it can certainly pay huge dividends in the long run and provide a sense of accomplishment. And, remember, you don't have to be an expert in all the trades associated with building and remodeling to coordinate your project successfully. The subcontractors are the experts in their fields. When you hire an HVAC contractor, you can assume they know how to install a certain kind of heating or air-conditioning system. That is the job of an HVAC contractor. If that subcontractor does not know what they are doing, then you need to find a new HVAC company anyway. The same principle applies to all the subcontractors involved in building a home from the ground up.

When it comes to permits, which will be covered in Chapter 2, owners can apply for all their own permits, and it is not as scary as you might think. In fact, if you are working with an architect, your architect can also submit all the paperwork and apply for the permits for you. Your architect can serve as a great resource during the process, guiding you with knowledge and even finding reputable subcontractors who can do the work (more about finding and hiring subcontractors in Chapter 3). Thanks to the wonders of the internet, it is easier than ever to research information, products, and ideas; find contractors and tradesmen; and get design ideas. YouTube has a video for just about anything, including just about every aspect of the building industry.

Lastly, the best reason to act as your own contractor, especially on a remodeling project, is that no one knows your home better than you, and no one cares about it more than you do, because it is your home and your money. Most contractors are not going to put the time and effort into a project that the homeowner would, worrying about every little detail and making sure everything is perfect, let alone take the time to research everything a homeowner might want. Most general contractors are in business to make money by building homes as quickly and cheaply as possible, then moving on to their next project. When I worked for a home builder many years ago, whenever a customer wanted to add or change something and the builder did not want to bother with it, he just killed it with price, meaning he would purposely give the customer a ridiculously high price for something he did not want to do, knowing full well the customer would just think it was too expensive and drop the idea. It can also be quite a process to change things with contractors, who often require change orders and charge fees for making simple changes, even changes that do not need an architect or subcontractor to do more work. Many contractors do this though they would never do it on a home they were building for themselves. Reputable contractors who build custom homes are often the exception to this because they are used to building homes with many extras and unique features that cookie-cutter builders and remodelers might not have experience installing. The bottom line is that a homeowner needs to find an architect and contractor who are flexible and willing to go the extra mile for their customer, even if it means putting the extra time and effort into researching materials, methods, and ideas with which they are not familiar.

As a homeowner acting as your own contractor, you will have the knowledge to make the decisions that are best for you based on your wants, needs, and priorities, not someone else's. Many contractors are not even familiar with many home products on the market today if they are items they do not usually include in a home. If you want a steam room, radiant floor heat, towel warmers, a dumbwaiter, an elevator, secret doorways, or other specialty items that are actually increasing in popularity, you do not want your contractor brushing off your requests or not taking you seriously just because they are not familiar with certain products. This happened to me many times, which was another reason I decided to act as my own contractor. I figured if I knew more about certain products I wanted in my home than the contractor, there was a problem. If I had to spend hours and hours of my own time researching things, why should I pay a contractor to do what I was already doing?

In short, acting as your own contractor gives you complete control over the project and, with some research, possibly makes you more knowledgeable about the things you want in your home than many contractors. If in the end you decide to work with a contractor on your project, this book can still provide you with a wealth of knowledge that is sure to make you a more informed client who is better able to control costs and make your project progress more smoothly with fewer surprises and headaches. If you do decide to hire a general contractor, you should apply the same diligence to choosing one as you would if acting alone and hiring all the subcontractors yourself.

Hiring a Contractor or Acting Alone

Benjamin Franklin is often credited with inventing the T-chart to help him make important decisions. There is also a closing technique many salesmen use called the Ben Franklin close, based on the same principle. Let's use Ben Franklin's strategy on the next page to review the reasons for acting as your own contractor and those for hiring a general contractor.

Acting as Your Own Contractor	Hiring a General Contractor
Save money by eliminating contractor fees and markups	Money is not a factor
Control your expenses by knowing the true cost of materials and labor	Do not have the time or want to put forth the effort
Reinvest savings into your project	Want someone else to do all the work
Ability to make and prioritize decisions based on your needs	Do not like dealing with people and want someone else to take care of all the details
Ability to make changes quicker and easier	Do not want to deal with the day-to-day aspects of a construction project
Can hire a project manager to help you when you are not available	
Sense of pride and accomplishment	
Requires legwork to research and order products and materials, find and hire subcontractors, and be available to answer questions and make decisions over the course of the project	

Chapter 1
My Background

Setting goals is the first step in turning the invisible into the visible.

—Tony Robbins

Writing and home improvement have been part of my life for many years. This book grew out of my enjoyment of both. My first book detailed the history of the Beverly Hills and Morgan Park neighborhoods on Chicago's south side and was published by Arcadia Publishing in 2003 as part of their Images of America series. This book was fueled by a passion for architecture and history and an appreciation for the uniqueness of this urban enclave. The area is known to people in the community as the "Village in the City" because of the architectural richness of its housing stock and the strong community ties that often go back generations. It was the grandness and diversity of the neighborhood's architecture, with so many of the homes built during the late 1800s through the 1920s, that led to the neighborhood being listed on the National Register of Historic Places. The Tudor, Victorian, Spanish, Colonial, Georgian, and Prairie School-style homes, along with the mansions built along Longwood Drive atop the Blue Island Ridge, which is a moraine left over from the receding glaciers of the last Ice Age, fueled my interest in architecture and history. Many of the homes are protected by landmark status, but it was the tearing down of so many architectural gems in other parts of the city and the complete blandness and lack of quality of so many newer suburban homes that fueled my passion for preservation. While I have spent my adult life as a history teacher, these factors made me a fan of the TV show *This Old House* since its inception and instilled in me the desire to one day renovate a beautiful old house while maintaining its architectural and historical integrity.

A few years ago, I had the opportunity to do this when I moved back into my childhood home with my family after the passing of my mother and spent the next few years renovating the home, a 1929 Spanish

Revival complete with a stone turret, arched French doors, a cathedral ceiling, and a Spanish clay tile roof. Most people say the house looks like a castle, but to me it has always been home, and it was a dream of mine to raise my own family in this special house. It also allowed me the chance to engage in things I enjoy, such as planning, designing, and creating. In fact, my first career interest was in architecture. Then, after high school, I got accepted into the mechanical engineering program at the University of Illinois at Chicago but wound up pursuing a career in teaching history, another passion of mine, when I realized a career in engineering or architecture might mean designing things that other people wanted, rather than pursuing my own ideas and designs.

But the passion for architecture and engineering never went away and were put to good use in the renovation of my family home, culminating in a three-level addition that expanded, updated, and improved the ninety-year-old home. This book is about that journey and is hopefully presented in a way that allows the reader to benefit from my knowledge, experience, trials and errors, mistakes and successes, frustrations, and jubilations. It is also meant to show anyone thinking of building, remodeling, or expanding a home how to potentially save tens of thousands dollars without doing any of the physical labor themselves.

However, I did not go into this project completely cold. I received my real estate license when I was twenty-one years old, took a course on general contracting, and at one point worked as a new home consultant for a developer who built homes in a subdivision outside Chicago. When my wife and I bought a classic Chicago bungalow a few blocks from where I grew up, I spent a few years renovating that home, including stripping and staining a lot of the woodwork, remodeling the kitchen, refinishing the floors, and doing all the rough and trim carpentry in the basement we finished. It was all a preview of what was to come. After moving back to my childhood home, I also spent about two years researching every aspect of putting an addition on the house before we started. That being said, I am confident homeowners, house flippers, and even contractors will find the information in this book useful.

My Project

In both our home renovations, the Chicago bungalow and the 1929 Spanish Revival home where we built our addition, I made sure to use materials and design techniques that would complement the homes. In the case of the addition, I wanted it to match the existing house and maintain its architectural and historic integrity; I didn't want the addition to look like an addition. While money is always a factor, I knew from the start the upfront investment to make the addition look good on the outside as well as the inside would be well worth the investment. I had seen bad-looking additions and cared about the house and neighborhood enough that I decided from the start that if I couldn't do it right, I wouldn't do it at all. A major renovation and possible addition are things I had always dreamed of for many reasons, mostly because the forty-foot-long tandem garage that ran behind the house had been slowly falling down for decades. We did not start the addition until about three years after we moved in because there was so much other work that had to be done.

The basement had major water issues, the air-conditioning system had to be replaced, and virtually all the floors had to be redone. (Carpeting and 1960s parquet flooring had been installed over the original oak floors, and many years of cats urinating had ruined the floors in certain areas. When we pulled up the parquet flooring in the dining room, we actually found the wiring for the floor buzzer that would be pressed with a foot to call the servants into the dining room.) The roof had to be repaired in certain areas that had caused water damage inside, and a lot of wiring had to be replaced.

Not only was the garage falling down, but it also could not be repaired because we determined that it had been built without the proper footings, probably because it was right on the lot line. There was no saving the garage, and it was too narrow to get a modern car into anyway. The house is situated on a corner lot and actually has two driveways, one facing each of the two streets. The garage also had two doors, one at each end, so someone could drive in one driveway, come through the garage, and drive right out the other end without having to back up or turn around. This was probably because many 1920s-era cars did not go in reverse. In fact, some old homes had turntables in their garages to spin a car around. Yes, just like the Batcave!

The only way to make the garage wider was to eliminate the long gangway that ran between the house and the garage and attach a new garage to the house, but doing that would have blocked the back door to the home and cut off direct access to the backyard patio. It made no sense to rebuild the garage the way it was. Rebuilding the garage as part of a larger addition was the only thing that made any sense.

The new addition would solve another major problem: namely, the fact that the kitchen, which was in the rear of the house, was incredibly small. The house, like many homes in the area, was built during the boom times of the 1920s in what was then a very wealthy neighborhood full of large homes where many people had servants. The original kitchen was actually in the basement, where food was prepared by the help, who would then bring it upstairs to be served from a small serving area or butler's pantry. As times changed, the basement kitchen was turned into a laundry room, and the serving area upstairs became a very small kitchen with very little storage or countertop space or even room to move.

All the bedrooms had small closets, even in the large master bedroom, as was also common for older homes, and our clothes were located in closets all over the house. Our daughter's bedroom was the same small bedroom I grew up in, and while the master bedroom did have its own bathroom, it was small. Tearing down the garage, which had to be done anyway at some point, and rebuilding it as part of a larger addition with a new kitchen on the first level and a new master bedroom and master bath on the second level was what made the most sense. Since adding a basement area under the new kitchen would not cost that much more than digging out the same area for a crawl space, we decided to do that as well. In doing so, we cut from the new basement to the existing basement through a horrible old step-up bath that was never used and had to be redone anyway. We were able to simply move this bathroom over a bit and turn it into a small but nice new bathroom for the basement.

The old garage was built with solid brick, and the walls were three bricks thick. Rather than buy new bricks that would never match the existing house, we had the masons demolish the old garage by hand and clean and reuse the reclaimed bricks to build the new addition. We also extended the second-floor rear gable dormer over the new master bedroom and used matching Spanish clay tile roofing to tie the old and new roofs together in that area. Most people unfamiliar with the house would never know the rear of the home is an addition, and that was the objective. A moment of extreme pride occurred when I was asked to put the home on the annual Beverly Hills/Morgan Park home tour sponsored by the Beverly Area Planning Association. This book details all the work inside and out, from excavation and foundation up to the roof and all the machinal systems in between. It is my hope that this book will serve as a valuable guide to anyone thinking of building or renovating a home.

Pre–Construction Project Photographs

Figure 3. North view with driveway off the street, showing a slanting garage separated from the house by a gangway. The garage used to have clay tile overhangs over each door on the north and south sides that collapsed decades ago as the garage was falling down. The facades were repaired without the overhangs, but that did not solve the underlying issue of the garage continuing to lean away from the house due to inadequate footings when it was built.

Figure 4. This is the southern view of the garage from the patio, showing it slanting to the east, away from the house, and water damage to the bricks. This is where the addition would be built.

Figure 5. This large fissure shows the walls of the garage pulling away as the structure was falling away from the house. Water would get into the cracks and freeze in the winter. The ice would pop the bricks out even more during freezing and thawing cycles.

Figure 6. The forty-foot tandem garage ran behind the house along the rear lot line. The tiled gable roof on the back of the house would be extended over the new kitchen and bedroom area.

Figure 7. Demolition with bricks being cleaned and stacked so they can be reused. The concrete roof of the garage was supported with large jacks during demolition.

Figure 8. Notice the plywood protecting the rear windows of the house during construction and the thickness of the garage walls, which supplied more than enough bricks for the project.

Chapter 2
Getting Started

Impossible is just a word thrown around by small men who find it easier to live in the world they've been given than to explore the power they have to change it. Impossible is not a fact. It's an opinion. Impossible is potential. Impossible is temporary. Impossible is nothing.

—Muhammad Ali

In the immortal words of legendary Chicago architect Ludwig Mies van der Rohe, "God is in the details." Therefore, when it comes to completing a project on time, within budget, and with few setbacks, there is no substitute for a well-thought-out plan that encompasses everything that needs to be done and anticipates potential problems. This is well worth repeating to emphasize how critically important it is to have a well-conceived plan that is supported by logistical details. For example, you do not want to purchase your dream jacuzzi tub only to find out that your plumber put the drain in the wrong location for that specific tub because he was not told otherwise. And you do not want to decide that you want a garage heater or a towel warmer after it is too late for one to be installed. From time to time, this book will emphasize important points to remember through Builder Alerts like this:

> **Builder Alert: There is no substitute for a well-thought-out plan that encompasses everything that needs to be done and anticipates potential problems.**

Your Project

The first question many homeowners who are considering remodeling have to answer is if they would rather remodel, build an addition, or move. Many people decide just to buy a larger or more up-to-date home. Other people want to remodel what they already have, while still others want to expand their current home. Building a completely new house is not usually an option in older, more established communities, although in some areas, it has become quite common for people to tear down a home and build a new one. In many older communities where people want to remain, it is quite common for people to build an addition rather than to move out of the area or to a new development farther away. Everyone's situation, needs, and desires are different, and all have different social and economic factors that need to be considered. Generally speaking, renovations that include updating or expanding kitchens and baths and adding a bedroom yield the greatest return on investment in terms of resale value.

Another important factor homeowners have to think about is where they will live while their home is being built or remodeled. Most people can live through a basement or kitchen remodel, albeit with some inconvenience, but living through a major construction project brings its own set of challenges on top of the construction itself. Whether your family is willing and able to live through a remodel really depends on the nature and scope of the work being done and what other options exist.

Our project consisted of building an addition on the rear of the house. Almost all the major work was done outside until it was time to tie the plumbing, electrical, heating, and air conditioning into the existing home. After that, most of the work continued in the addition until it was time to cut through to the existing house. Before then, most of the noise and mess was close, but it was still outside. Once we cut through, things got really messy, and we had to deal with workers in the home on a constant basis. It was inconvenient to say the least, but most of the work was still relegated to only a few rooms in the house. If your project will consist of gutting the entire house or upending the living situation for the family, then moving out temporarily might be the only option. Of course, this involves moving in with family and storing your furniture somewhere or renting a house or apartment until you can move back. Aside from the inconvenience of moving and taking into consideration a new commute to work or school for your children, there is the added expense of paying rent for several months or more that must be factored into the overall budget of the project.

Living through the construction made the most sense for our project, but if you are considering doing this, I would strongly suggest setting aside money in your budget for a cleaning service and some local college kids to help with cleanup and to move things around as needed. It seemed like we were cleaning virtually all the time, and whenever it was time for a messy part of the project, such as drywall or cutting through masonry, the dust drifted all through the house again. Cleaning was a never-ending job.

Every time a different area of the home was affected by construction, we also had to move many items out of the way—the appliances, the bedroom furniture, whatever. It was a lot of work and took a lot of time. We also had to empty the garage before work began and were often taking things back and forth between home and the storage place we rented to keep things during construction. Therefore, definitely invest in the help of some college kids to move things around as needed and to help with selected demolition, such as ripping out cabinets or pulling up carpeting if you are acting as your own contractor. It is money I am sure they would be glad to have, and their help will save you and your family much time and effort.

If you are having a new home built but cannot qualify for a new construction loan until you sell your current house, you will either have to sell your current home and find a place to live until the new home is built or see if you can get a bridge loan. There is more information about bridge loans in Chapter 5, but if this is not a possibility, and you have to sell your current house first, then you will be in the same situation of having to move in with a family member or factor the cost of renting a place into your overall construction budget.

This book assumes the decision to move or remodel has already been made and focuses mostly on the remodeling and addition scenarios, but the principles and ideas in this book apply very much to building a home from the ground up. In fact, many home additions incorporate all the same principles and work required to build a new home, just on a smaller scale.

When building a new home, however, it is important to note that some land developers require that only certain builders be used, especially if the builder is also the one selling the lots. But if the developer in a new subdivision allows buyers to use whatever builder they want, you can just as easily employ the information in the book to act as your own general contractor. However, it is imperative that you check with the property developer or builder selling the land to find out what their building guidelines are. Check with the local municipality to see what their restrictions and requirements are regarding homeowners acting as their own general contractors. It is common for developers of a subdivision to require homes to be built to certain specifications. These restrictive covenants, as they are known, specify such things as minimum square footage, height, style, color schemes, building materials, landscaping, setbacks, the building of pools or fences, special assessments, and many other items the builder and homeowner must know. This information is contained in the developer's or homeowners association's covenants, conditions, and restrictions documentation. These CC&Rs, as they are commonly known, specify certain rules homeowners must follow in the building and use of their property. You don't want to build your dream home only to find out later that you are not allowed to have a pool or fence, so do your due diligence in researching this information.

> **Builder Alert: When buying undeveloped land, it is imperative that you check with the property developer or builder to find out what their building guidelines are and with the local municipality to see what their restrictions and requirements are regarding homeowners acting as the general contractor.**

When building a new home, it is also important to find out which banks and lending institutions finance the purchase of land and give construction loans to homeowners acting as their own general contractor. Many banks will finance the sale of land if it is in conjunction with the building of a home, but many banks will not finance land sales alone, as in the case of someone wanting to purchase a lot now to build on it at a later date. Other lenders might require 50 percent down or have other financing requirements because land sales are considered riskier. While it has become more common for people to act as their own contractors, some lenders still prefer that the homeowner use a licensed contractor to avoid cost overruns that could adversely affect the cost of the project and therefore the final loan amount. If the total cost of a project turns out to be greater than the borrower was initially approved for, and therefore they can no longer afford the loan, the lender could be stuck with an unfinished home. That is a situation the lender wants to avoid.

This all seems somewhat counterintuitive because the main reason for a homeowner to act as their own contractor is to save money, thereby keeping the costs down in the first place, but lenders are concerned about risk and making sure a project does not get away from the homeowner to the point of jeopardizing the loan through cost overruns. Many banks have no restrictions on homeowners acting as the general contractor, but some do, so it is still best to find out ahead of time. There is more information about financing your project in Chapter 5.

Assuming you have decided on whether you are remodeling, building an addition, or building a new home, it is time to start putting together a plan. Many midsize homes built in the last thirty years incorporate new features current homeowners desire, such as a large kitchen, an open floor plan, a family room, and more closet space, so remodeling might just consist of updating the house. Many people with much older homes, however, want not only to update their home but also to build an addition the includes a family room, a bigger kitchen, and/or new master suite. Owners of single-story ranch homes often choose to add a second floor or turn attic space into living space. Dark, damp, dreary basements are also being replaced by finished basements that can add a considerable amount of space and are just as nice as the finished spaces on the main level.

Whatever type of project you decide is right for your family, your construction project will be limited by the building and zoning codes that apply to your property, which detail what can be built and what size structure is allowed.

Site Plan

If you are building onto an existing home, building in a new subdivision, or replacing a teardown with a new home, the size and shape of the lot, the location of utilities and easements, and the zoning setbacks (how far away from the lot lines a structure must be located) will greatly determine the site plan and how any new structures will be situated. There are many details that must be considered when planning the site, so spend some time going over them all with your architect. If you are building on a large piece of land that allows a great deal more freedom of design, you and the architect should consider other factors, such as drainage patterns and flood control; directional setting to maximize or minimize exposure to the sun and wind in certain rooms and outside areas; location of shaded and shadowed areas; location of sewer lines and other utilities; location of the driveway, garage, and other outbuildings; placement of a well and septic tank if required; and the desired landscaping. If you want to make use of solar power, the placement of the solar panels will certainly affect the overall design to maximize the exposure to the sun. The topography of the land will be important if you want a certain view or a walkout basement. Land that is hilly might provide unique building opportunities but also might require a great deal more site preparation. It is also important to know how far away utilities such as water, sewer, electric, cable, and telephone lines are located from undeveloped land and how much it will cost to bring those utilities to your property.

In rural areas, it is also important to know the source of your water. Will your property have municipal water and sewer connections? Will you need a private well for your water? Does the well tap into an underground aquifer that many other people use for house water or agricultural irrigation that might be in danger of going dry at some point? Water rights are technically known as riparian rights and are a must-know for prospective homeowners.

Most importantly, when buying undeveloped land, especially in rural areas, make sure you are legally allowed to build a home on that property and that it is not located in a wash or flood plain. And make sure there is unrestricted access to the property via a public road or drive that is not owned by someone else. Believe it or not, there are plenty of examples of people who bought or invested in property that was unbuildable for legal or practical reasons or required a tremendous amount of work and money to correct site problems. Lots have also been sold to which there was no direct access except over someone else's property. Use due diligence in researching undeveloped land before buying, especially if the price seems too good to be true. It is well worth hiring a lawyer to perform a title search and research the building guidelines for undeveloped land. Other factors to consider include the cost of building your home compared to the current market value of similar homes in the area. You might not want to spend $500,000 building a home in an area where the average price of a similar house is only $300,000 as you might not recoup your investment if you ever sell the home. In all these cases, an ounce of prevention is certainly worth a pound of cure.

Builder Alert: When buying undeveloped land, make sure you are legally allowed to build a home on the property, and there is unrestricted access to the property via a public road or drive that is not owned by someone else.

Locating Utilities

If you are building an addition or even performing any type of major relandscaping, it is necessary to hire a service to locate and mark all the underground utilities. The last thing you want to do is break a water, sewer, or electrical line, and of course, breaking a gas line could be catastrophic. Illinois has a free service for homeowners and contractors: Joint Utility Locating Information for Excavators (JULIE). Other states and localities offer similar services. Once you call them, they will come out pretty quickly to locate and mark all underground utilities, using their access to municipal records and their own electronic locators to mark the path of the utility lines from the street to the house. You will have to call your local utility companies if any utility lines need to be moved.

Builder Alert: Hire a service to locate and mark all underground utilities.

When planning an addition, it is important to figure out where the sewer line runs out of the house and whether any gutter downspouts or yard drains connect to the sewer. Figuring this out is not always easy, especially for corner houses where the sewer line might connect to the sewer main under either street. It is also important to figure out how the plumbing for a new kitchen or bathroom will connect to the existing sewer system or if a new sewer line has to be run to the sewer main. Figuring this out ahead of time is a necessity, so it is worth bringing in a plumber with a camera to map out the sewer pipes and other connections to develop a plan the architect and excavators can follow. Chicago has a combined sewer system, meaning rainwater and sewage flow into the same sewer. Other municipalities separate their sewer lines, so it is important to know the building requirements in your locale.

Many older homes also have catch basins located somewhere on the property, usually in the rear of the home or near the kitchen. These usually look like a round sewer with a black or red metal lid surrounded by a concrete ring and are several feet deep with a sewer intake pipe. Catch basins were originally used as large grease traps to keep grease poured down the kitchen sink from flowing into the sewer. Catch basins are no longer required in many municipalities and can be eliminated by rerouting the lines that drain into them. (Again, check your building codes, and if you have a catch basin, it is a good idea to have it cleaned out once in a great while if you do not remove it.)

The ability to eliminate a catch basin is good news, considering they are often located in the rear of homes where many additions are built. It was also a blessing in disguise for us because it made for easy access to the sewer line when building our addition. However, it is important to know if anything else besides the kitchen sink drains into the basin. In our rear addition project, the old garage drains, a patio drain, and a couple of downspout drains all ran below ground and emptied into the catch basin that was located between the house and the garage. The gutter downspouts no longer flowed into the ground drains anyway as I removed them as a precaution against backups and water infiltration into the basement via old, cracked drain pipes. Only the patio drain had to be rerouted. When the area was excavated, the concrete-and-brick catch basin was simply removed, but the sewer line remained in place, where it was easily connected to the new sewer lines for the addition before the new foundation was poured. The addition also has access points that serve as clean-outs, so we can rod out the sewer lines when needed.

Building Wish List

Whether you are building a new home, remodeling, or building an addition, your plan must contain a wish list. The reality is that most people can't afford everything they want, but having a wish list allows you to keep track of things, plan a budget, and prioritize items. This might be your only chance to build a home or an addition, so it is important to get it right the first time, with no regrets. Certain things can be added at a later date; other things have to be included from the start.

For example, granite countertops look great, hold up well, and add resale value to a home. However, they are also an expensive upgrade to a kitchen, often costing several thousands of dollars. It is common to spend $5,000 or more on these countertops. But what if you also really want a new gas fireplace that also costs about the same amount of money? If you have to choose, go with the fireplace now. You can easily upgrade the countertops anytime in the future when you have more money, but the fireplace has to be planned for from the beginning.

If you don't have the money for something now and might want it later but are worried about having to tear things apart to make these improvements, certain things can be planned out ahead of time to make future installation much easier. If you are having a new house or addition built but are not ready to finish the basement, you can easily have the plumbing for a possible future bathroom "roughed in." This means installing the water and sewer lines at the time of building so that they can easily be connected without having to hack up the basement floor at a later date. The concept holds true for a variety of scenarios, such as garage heaters, an outdoor gas line for a gas grill, connections for a steam shower or towel warmer, audio/visual hookups for a home theater, et cetera. All these upgrades can easily be added at a later date with some advanced planning, so if money is an issue, save it for things that must be completed at the time of building.

Therefore, it is a good idea to start with a wish list of everything you would like, then work backward to prioritize items based on your wants, needs, and budget. It's also important to communicate all your desires to your architect. The following wish list contains some items popular in new homes and remodeling projects.

Wish List

1. Radiant floor heat
2. Outside stairs to basement
3. Basement bathroom
4. Walk-in pantry
5. First-floor laundry room
6. Central Vacuum system
7. Outdoor gas line for grill or fireplace (check codes)
8. Water lines for ice maker and water dispenser
9. Garage heater
10. Fireplace (chimney for wood burning)
11. Steam shower and jacuzzi tub
12. Granite/quartz countertops
13. Towel warmer
14. Home theater
15. Intercom/video doorbell system
16. Security/surveillance system
17. Elevator/dumbwaiter
18. Underground sprinkler system
19. Home gym/swim spa
20. Closet organizer system

Working with an Architect

While kitchen and other simple remodeling projects don't usually require the use of an architect, building a custom home or an addition will, and the architect will likely be the most important person you choose for your project. Expect to pay several thousand dollars to an architect for his or her time. The bigger the project, the more detail involved, and the more you will pay.

When choosing an architect, it is important to find someone who is knowledgeable and experienced in projects like yours and in your location. It is important that the architect is aware of the local building codes, zoning requirements, and permit process and has a good working relationship with the local authorities who might be needed to approve your project. If your home is located in a historic district, be sure your architect is aware of any and all provisions that might be required for building or remodeling in such an area. Find an architect who can design a home or addition that fits the style of the rest of the neighborhood and matches the existing home. For an addition, make sure the architect can tie in the new roof to the old and design the addition with matching characteristics and proper proportions, so the new structure is aesthetically pleasing as well as functional. The architect should also be familiar with the submission and approval process for the local preservation organization and hopefully have a relationship with the people working there.

All these factors will help the project progress faster, smoother, and with fewer setbacks. The architect can also be a great source of subcontractors and other tradesmen you might need for your project. When hiring an architect, be sure to ask for references from past customers and details of previous projects similar to yours, including photographs and addresses. The best ways to find an architect are via word of mouth and signs for other construction projects in the area. Architects and builders often display their signs on jobsites, so if you like what you see, this can be a great place to start. The internet can also be a good place to locate architects in a particular area, but referrals from neighbors or nearby homeowners who built a house or addition are usually the best place to start.

When hiring an architect, make sure you explain exactly what you are looking for, both in your project and in the services you expect. If it is not the right fit, do not be afraid to walk away and find someone else. If you are going to act as your own general contractor, be sure to explain this and ask if the architect has experience with this situation and is open to it. When acting as your own general contractor, you will have to use an architect who is knowledgeable about the self-certification process. In Chicago, architects must complete training and obtain a "self-cert" certificate since the "architect of record" takes full responsibility for code compliance. Make sure the architect you choose is aware of any such requirement in your municipality and has obtained any necessary approvals to work on an owner self-certification project. The city of Chicago actually has a list of certified "self-cert" architects on its building department website.

> **Builder Alert: When self-certifying, the "architect of record" assumes full responsibility for compliance with building codes. Some municipalities, such as Chicago, require architects to attend self-certification training and obtain a self-certification certificate. Make sure your architect is aware of this and has completed the "self-cert" process.**

Acting as your own contractor can require more time and effort on the part of the architect to help you, so make sure the architect is fine with this. Also, find someone who is not only knowledgeable but also open to taking ideas and suggestions from a homeowner who might want to change things as the process moves along. In short, if you are a detail-oriented person and know exactly how you want things, make sure your architect is OK with taking cues from you and does not simply want to do what is fastest or easiest for him or her.

The architect will no doubt have a contract for you to sign. Make sure everything you expect is outlined in the contract and what, if any, the charges are for extra services, such as submitting paperwork and applying for permits, meeting with subcontractors, attending zoning meetings, et cetera. Generally, the architect will bill you on an hourly rate for his or her services, including the drawing up of the blueprints and any other work to be done afterward. Once the work has been approved, the permits issued, and the construction started, any time the architect spends on your project will likely be consulting with you and the subcontractors "in the field." See if you can negotiate a lower hourly rate for this aspect of the job than you paid to have all the plans drawn up and submitted. The more you know what you want in your project upfront, the less money you will pay the architect to make changes to your plans.

Before you begin, the first order of business will be obtaining a survey of your property. You should have this done before you hire the architect. The architect will need this because it shows the size of the property, along with the lot lines. With knowledge of the building codes, the zoning requirements, and the accompanying requirements for setbacks, the architect will know what can be built; what cannot be built; and what needs special permission, such as a zoning approval, to be built. You also have to submit a survey with the architect's blueprints as part of the permit process. Reputable companies can perform a standard residential survey for a few hundred dollars.

Before an architect starts working on blueprints for an addition, he or she must have a detailed set of plans for how the house looks now, called "as-built" plans. For these plans, the architect has to take extremely detailed measurements of every aspect of the existing house to produce a set of blueprints that details exactly how the house looks in its current state, down to all the doors and windows, how tall they are, and how far apart they are. These drawings also have to be submitted alongside the drawings for the proposed addition. Since this is a time-consuming and therefore costly part of the process, see if your architect uses a draftsperson or interior architect for this part of the job. These are basically people who are quite capable of taking the same measurements and doing the same drawings but are not full-fledged architects and, therefore, charge a great deal less money for their services. You might be able to find someone like this on your own, but make sure your architect will accept another person's work. Lastly, you will need a completed set of blueprints from the architect before you can begin getting bids from general contractors, subcontractors, and materials suppliers. They will all base their estimates on the blueprints.

Historic Designations

If your home is a designated landmark or sits within a national, state, or local historic district, you could be restricted in what you are able to do regarding demolition and construction. While some historic designations are primarily symbolic, others are overseen by historic preservation organizations that might have to approve any structural changes. You could be prohibited from tearing down a home and have to adhere to strict architectural or historical guidelines when building, remodeling, or expanding a home. It is best to do your due diligence first to make sure your property does not reside in any type of historic district, and if it does, to know what alterations you are allowed to make. If this is the case, your architect will need to know what guidelines he or she must follow because your building permit might be contingent on the review and approval of your plans by the preservation organization that works in conjunction with your municipality. In Chicago, the Commission on Landmarks is staffed by the Historic Preservation Division of the Department of Planning and Development. They review proposed demolitions and alterations to structures that are considered historically or architecturally significant or that lie within the boundaries of a landmark district. Homeowners can enter their address into the Chicago Department of Planning and Development's online zoning map to see if their home is a designated landmark or lies within a landmark district. Look for the same type of information and resources in your location. A local architect should be able to find this type of information easily.

Building Permits

If you will be using a general contractor, this person will be the one applying for all the construction permits. You will be charged for the permit application fees and the time the contractor spends submitting all the necessary paperwork. This is part of the fee they charge for their work. The cost of the building permit is usually determined by the nature and scope of the project and also covers any necessary inspections. It is best to check with your local municipality to find out the permit fees in your area, but expect to spend several hundred to over a thousand dollars on a permit for a new home or addition. Also, some municipalities might charge what is commonly known as an impact fee. The is a fee to offset the cost, or impact, your project might have on the community's infrastructure and budget if it's determined that your project will lead to increased expenses related to improving roads, sewer and water lines, traffic lights, and municipal services such as additional schools, parks, or police and fire protection. Impact fees are one-time fees, usually based on the square footage of the home, and can range from a few hundred to a few thousand dollars, which will be added to the cost of your initial building permit.

For example, the city of Chicago has an open-space impact fee for new residential developments to pay for land acquisition and park improvements in all the city's community areas. The fees currently range from $313 to $1,253. Check with your local municipality to see if they charge impact fees, if they apply to the replacing of an existing home that is being torn down, and if they apply to owners of new single-family homes or only to developers building multiple dwellings.

If you are acting as your own contractor, your architect will apply for the permits that allow you to self-certify, or act as the general contractor. In doing this, the architect of record assumes full responsibility for code compliance. Some municipalities require architects to attend self-certification training and obtain a self-certification certificate. Make sure your architect is aware of this and has completed the self-cert process. The city of Chicago actually has a list of self-cert architects on their building department website, as well as lists of all contractors licensed to work in the city. It is a good idea to become familiar with your municipality's online resources. Resources like this allow you to make sure a contractor is licensed, follow the permit application and review process, and even schedule your building inspections.

The permit forms are not terribly complicated, but it is definitely better to have your architect complete and submit them and then reimburse the architect for his time and the permit fees. The permit is not one form but a series of documents related to various aspects of the process. Combined, all the documents make up what is known as the standard plan review.

The permit process, fees, and application can vary dramatically from one municipality to the next, as can the time it takes to receive an approval or denial letter. You might have to submit a copy of your deed of ownership of the property to prove you are the person legally allowed to authorize the work being done. You will probably also have to include a recent survey of the property. In Chicago, you cannot obtain a building permit if you owe the city any debts. Yes, there is a form the homeowner has to fill out that states they do not owe the city any money, such as outstanding parking tickets, and there is a debt clearance form to prove that any debts have been satisfied.

You will most likely have to include the names, license numbers, and possibly the liability insurance policy numbers of certain subcontractors you will use on the permit application. Sometimes the electrical contractor will be required to pull a separate permit for the electrical work. The subcontractor information you will have to include on the application only pertains to the work the municipality requires be done by licensed contractors, such as the electrical work and excavation.

In Chicago, the city itself has to be named as an additional insured party on the excavation contractor's general liability policy for the amount of $1 million if the homeowner is acting as the general contractor. In Chicago, the self-cert actually lists the homeowner as the plumber, so no specific subcontractor information is required for plumbing. Again, the permit process and application vary from location to location, so make sure your architect is familiar with your local permitting process. The forms can usually be downloaded from the municipality's website. Some municipalities allow all the paperwork to be completed and uploaded online with all the necessary supporting documents and blueprints.

If you are tearing down a house to build a new one, you will need a separate demolition permit. It is also extremely important to remember that you cannot tear down a house with a mortgage on it to build a new house unless the mortgage company is aware of your plan. You have to get their permission to do this, and since you will probably be getting a construction loan for the new project, the bank will be part of this process anyway. But the bottom line is that if you have a mortgage on a house, the bank is still an owner until the mortgage is paid off, and you cannot tear it down without their knowledge and written consent.

Builder Alert: If you plan to tear down your existing house and replace it with a new one, you will need written approval from your mortgage company.

It is a great idea to obtain the permit application information far in advance so that you can become familiar with the information you will need to obtain. Once you obtain your permit, you will have to keep it posted and visually displayed in a prominent location until the completion of your project. If you make any major changes to your project, you will have to submit an amended application. If approved, you will be issued another permit. In short, the description outlined in your application and listed on your permit must correspond to the work being done. If you decide to add a second story or basement to your addition, for example, you and your architect have to submit the necessary paperwork to include the changes. If the changes are in line with the local building and zoning codes, the changes should be approved. If the changes are not in line with those codes, the project could be delayed while the necessary approvals are obtained. Make sure you plan for everything the first time around to avoid any delays. You will also be charged a fee to submit changes.

Residential elevators and dumbwaiters are becoming more popular as technology has made it possible to install these products in a variety of spaces and for less money than in the past, allowing homeowners to "age in place." These are more cost effective if planned as part of a new home or addition rather than trying to retrofit them, though newer pneumatic vacuum elevators make retrofitting elevators in tight spaces easier. However, these devices require what are often known as an elevator/conveyance device installation permit.

Some municipalities also offer an "easy permit" for smaller projects that do not require architectural blueprints. This is a simpler and more streamlined process. Check with your local municipality regarding all permit options, requirements, and forms. Below is a simple checklist of what information you might need when applying for a permit. This list is not all encompassing. For Chicago residents, a complete list of all required self-cert information and documents can be found on the city's permit application website. Check with your local municipality for the same type of information.

Sample Information Needed for a Building Permit

1. A certified self-cert architect if not using a general contractor
2. Blueprints with site plan, elevations, and mechanical systems
3. Property information/ownership deed to property
4. Complete plat survey of property
5. Information and license number for electrical contractor
6. License and insurance information for excavation contractor
7. Zoning approval if required
8. Driveway application if required
9. Municipal/aldermanic acknowledgment letter
10. All other forms and documentation required, signed and completed, including debt check form

Building and Zoning Codes

Building codes are enacted to protect people from poor construction methods and unsafe materials and to provide equal access to people with disabilities. The codes vary greatly between residential and commercial structures and from locale to locale, but they are put into place for everyone's safety and need to be followed; otherwise, your property will not pass inspection. This could delay your project, and violations could be expensive to remedy once construction has already started. Examples of some basic building code requirements might include the width of doorways, the use of ground fault interrupter (GFI) outlets where required, the fire rating of certain doors, smoke alarms, height of light switches in handicap-accessible areas, fireproofing of all vertical penetrations (openings) between floors, height of fencing around pools, height of railings on a balcony, et cetera.

There are countless codes that regulate the building of structures. If you use a general contractor, they should be familiar with the building codes where the work is being performed. The subcontractors should be aware of the various building codes where they are working as well. If you are acting as your own contractor and self-certifying your project, your architect takes responsibility for everything being built according to code. The architect should be familiar with the local building codes and should incorporate the codes into the design of your home or addition, even if you are not self-certifying. Still, as the homeowner, it is a good idea to become familiar with some of the building codes. Your local municipality should have a copy of the building codes available online. If you can't find them, call your municipality to find out how you can obtain a hard or digital copy.

Zoning codes regulate the use of land. These codes specify what is allowed to be built on a certain piece of land and how it can be situated on the land. Zoning codes were adopted to protect land and neighbors from hazards and unwanted use that might interfere with the quality of life or value of nearby property. This is to protect neighbors, for example, from someone tearing down a house and erecting a tall apartment building, tearing down a few homes to build a gas station or factory, or keeping certain farm animals on their property. The list of zoning codes and possible violations is long, but zoning codes are important when buying land, building a home, or building an addition because you have to make sure that what you want to do is allowed under the current zoning conditions for a particular piece of property. If you want to build a house, make sure it is zoned single-family residential; if you want to raise farm animals on your land, make sure it is zoned for that.

Most people building a home or addition will be doing so on land that is already zoned for residential use. However, zoning codes can also regulate the size and height of structures. Some developments, especially those that offer unique views, are only zoned for single-story ranch homes with maximum height limits. When building a home or addition, the most common zoning rules are related to the size, height, and distance from property lines of the new structure. If your new structure does not conform to these zoning rules, your building permit will be denied unless you seek and are approved for a zoning change or variance.

Builder Alert: When building a home or addition, the most common zoning rules are related to the size, height, and distance from the property lines of the new structure.

The homeowner, architect, or general contractor must be aware of any height limitations and setback guidelines. Setbacks dictate how far away from the lot line a structure must be built. There are even different setback guidelines for the front, rear, and sides of a property. A set number can be used for a setback, such as three feet. Other times, a formula might be used to determine the setbacks for individual homes based on a percentage of the size of the lot, the size of the existing or proposed structure, the average front setback of other homes on the block, et cetera. The guidelines vary, so it is imperative that you and your architecture know the legal setbacks for your particular property as this could determine the size, shape, and placement of the new structure. The most common issues arise when a new home or addition is planned for a small lot, and the proposed structure will not fit within the current setbacks. If your design does not fall within the given setbacks, you will have to redesign your project for zoning approval unless granted a zoning change. This is why a survey of the property must be included in the building permit application.

Zoning Changes

Just because the design of your new home or addition does not meet the current zoning guidelines for a new structure, all hope is not lost. It is quite common to seek a zoning change that will allow you to build your home or addition. Zoning changes are typically requested when someone wants to change the use of the land, say from residential to commercial or from single family to multi-family. These can be complicated endeavors because they often have economic, social, and political ramifications that must be considered. Zoning changes that allow a new home or addition to encroach on standard property line setbacks are quite common and not terribly complicated, though the zoning change process can be the same as when requesting a zoning change for land use.

In Chicago, there two types of zoning changes that can be requested related to setbacks. If the proposed new home or addition requires slight adjustments to the zoning code that do not materially affect the surrounding properties, the homeowner can apply for what is known as an administrative adjustment. There is a fee for this ($500 at the time of this writing), and it is meant to provide a faster and more streamlined process for minor zoning adjustments. In Chicago, even though there are setbacks for all properties, it is permissible to build right up to the lot line under certain conditions. If major changes such as this are needed, the homeowner will need to apply for a full-blown zoning variance. This is precisely what we had to do on our project because the garage was right on the rear lot line, and the project called for taking down the garage and rebuilding it as part of the new addition on the back of the house. Our garage, like so many other garages built at the time, was built at the rear of the house and right up to the lot line, so there was no place else to go.

Since the house would not meet current zoning setback guidelines, the only hope for our project was a variance allowing us to build or, in this case, rebuild right up to the lot line, and in doing so, turn formerly nonliving space into living space. If we were not allowed to do this, we would not have gone ahead with our addition the way we wanted.

The zoning variance request took months to be approved because of the backlog of cases the city had to process and the fact that the zoning board of appeals only met once per month to hear cases. We also had to apply for the building permit first, knowing it would be denied, then submit the denial letter from the building department to the zoning department with the request for a variance. This was a long and expensive process that took about six months to complete and required the use of a zoning attorney. At the time, the filing fee for a zoning change was $500, but there were many other costs involved, including a title search, ethics fee, and mailing expenses. When all was said and done, the total cost of our zoning request was around $4,000, including the attorney fees, which comprised the bulk of the expense.

The variance guidelines also required notifying all the neighbors in a certain radius of our property of our proposed project and serving public notice once a hearing date was scheduled with the zoning board of appeals so anyone who might have objections could voice their concerns. We had a good relationship with all the neighbors, and everyone knew our garage was falling down, so fortunately, no issues came up during the process. We also had a signed letter from our alderman, voicing his support for the project. In Chicago, this can make or break a project, but in any situation, you would be well advised to have all your ducks in a row from the start. Too many objections or a neighbor who has a beef with you could derail the project, so it is best to be honest and upfront with your neighbors about your plans from the start and keep them apprised of the variance process, so they are not caught off guard or worried when they start getting letters from your zoning attorney or see that Public Notice sign on your home.

On the date of the hearing, my architect, the zoning attorney, and I had to appear before the zoning board of appeals, explain the project, and state our case. The project was quickly approved a few days later, but we had to go through the same variance process as more complicated land-use proposals. While the zoning attorney assured us when we first met that this was a fairly common zoning request and thought it would be approved, there are no guarantees, and every situation might be different, so it is imperative that you learn whether or not the home or addition you are planning meets the zoning requirements for your lot; what the process is for requesting changes; and if those changes, even if approved, will meet your needs. If your addition needs fifteen feet and the most you might be able to gain from a zoning adjustment is only another ten feet, you and your architect will probably have to rethink your design.

When compared to the overall cost of the project, our zoning variance was a justified and necessary step toward getting our addition built the way we wanted. The process and cost can vary greatly from one location to another, so check with your municipality if you or your architect think your project might require some type of zoning change.

Inspections

If you are having a new home built, putting on an addition, or doing any other project that requires significant structural or mechanical work, you will undoubtably have to have the work inspected along the way and upon completion. Part of the permit fee covers the cost of these inspections, and the homeowner or general contractor must make sure the inspections are completed in a proper and timely manner. Failure to do so can greatly delay a project.

Inspections are required to make sure that the structure is being built safely and that all building codes are met. This is a good thing, so do not view the inspections as a necessary evil but as a way to ensure the work is done properly and that safe and smart building practices are used. Many contractors dread the inspection process, fearing any potential violations will cost time and money, especially because they fear an inspector might be too "picky."

This is the wrong attitude. Inspections are meant to protect the homeowner and ensure everyone's safety long after the building process is complete. This is something contractors should actually welcome should any potential problems be caught and corrected rather than being sued down the line by the homeowner if something goes wrong. While I had always heard of inspectors delaying projects because they did not like what they saw, I actually had a very positive experience with the inspectors on our project. I found them to be knowledgeable, helpful, and genuinely interested in looking out for me, the homeowner. They knew I was acting as my own general contractor and were more than willing to offer advice on all manner of construction-related items. All the inspections went smoothly, and we passed each inspection on the first try. If I had been a general contractor building a home for someone else, the dynamic might have been different. The inspector's job is to look out for the homeowner, not the contractor. In that case, inspectors might be less forgiving or patient when approving work if they suspect the general contractor might be cutting corners or doing a poor job at the homeowner's expense. In either case, when it comes to the inspections, the best defense is a good offense. That means making sure your subcontractors are aware of any and all building codes for your municipality and follow your architect's instructions and blueprints. If building codes are followed and accompanied by careful workmanship, there should be no problems, and the inspectors will have no reason to find fault with anything in the first place.

Depending on the requirements of your municipality and the scope of your project, you will have to schedule inspections throughout the building process as different phases are completed. Common inspections include:

- after the site is staked for excavation;
- after excavation is complete;

- after the sewer and underground utilities are laid;
- after the footings are poured;
- after the rest of foundation is poured;
- after the masonry is complete;
- after rough framing is complete;
- after rough plumbing is complete;
- after rough electrical is complete;
- the final plumbing inspection;
- the final electrical inspection; and
- the final occupancy inspection.

It is a good idea to schedule inspections for when you think the work will be completed instead of waiting for work to be done. Try to get a good estimate from the subcontractor as to when they think the work will be completed before inspection. This is because, depending on how busy the inspectors are, it might take a few weeks to get one scheduled. Get an idea of when the work will be done and schedule a date; if the work is delayed, you can reschedule the inspection. Time spent sitting around waiting for an inspection is lost time. If you lose a few weeks each time you need an inspection, the project could drag out longer than necessary. Your subcontractors will have to wait until each phase of the project passes inspection before they can proceed in case something has to be changed. Contractors do not like downtime either as that is time they could be spending working or moving on to another job, so plan ahead when it comes time for the inspections.

It is also a good idea to have your architect and pertinent subcontractors with you when you meet with the inspectors in case an inspector has any specific questions. Again, if the work is done properly, there should be no problems, but here is a list of several items various inspectors will definitely be looking for in a new home or addition (depending on local codes):

- GFI outlets in areas near water sources, such as in kitchens and baths;
- smoke detectors;
- firestops in rough framing;
- black pipe for gas lines;
- fire caulking of all vertical penetrations;
- spacing and size of floor joists;

- no notching or holes in floor joists;
- no HVAC return vents in bathrooms or kitchen;
- no HVAC vents in attached garages;
- no HVAC units or ductwork in garage unless allowed by code;
- fire-rated doors and windows where required by code;
- proper gauge wiring and circuit breakers;
- proper venting for plumbing system;
- proper size of foundational footings;
- drain tile, sump pump, and ejector pump if required;
- weep holes and control and expansion joints in concrete and masonry; and
- proper size pipes and required shut-off valves for gas and water pipes.

Again, if you make sure all building codes are followed, there should be no problems with the inspections.

Lead, Mold, and Asbestos Abatement

When remodeling older homes, lead-based paint, mold, and asbestos are common problems, and they are best solved by hiring a professional licensed in the abatement of these materials.

Lead-based paint was used until 1978, when it was banned for residential use. However, it is still common in many old homes. The common answer to lead-based paint was to cover it with new paint, thereby completely sealing it. Any renovation in which lead paint is suspected has to follow certain criteria to make sure lead flakes and dust are captured. Please research and follow prescribed guidelines when working in areas where lead paint is suspected. Contractors might require a disclosure form that outlines their work where lead paint is involved, such as wearing protective clothing, masks, and eye protection; using drop cloths; and following proper disposal guidelines. They might even charge extra for this.

Mold can cause serious breathing and lung problems to the inhabitants of a home. Mold grows in areas where water or moisture is common, such as in the basement, behind walls, or under flooring where water accumulates from seepage, leaky pipes, or holes in the roof. Sometimes you don't know mold is present until drywall or plaster is removed, but be aware of the potential for mold wherever water or dampness is common. All areas of mold growth must be removed. Do not delay; the longer the mold remains, the more spores will grow and spread. Severe cases could cost several hundred to several thousand dollars to remediate properly.

When in doubt, especially if mold is suspected, hire a mold inspector who is a certified industrial hygienist (CIH) or council-certified indoor environmental consultant (CIEC). The inspector might conduct air-quality tests and even remove part of a wall. If the situation does not look severe, the mold inspector might be able to tell you what steps they can take to solve the problem, such as removing the mold-infested materials and disinfecting the surrounding areas.

Asbestos is a carcinogen and was, unfortunately, a common building material for decades. In homes, asbestos-containing materials were in use through the 1970s. The most common uses of asbestos were in insulation and flooring. If the materials are disturbed or damaged, asbestos fibers can contaminate the air. Vermiculite was an asbestos-made insulation used in attics in some parts of the country. Make sure any attic insulation does not contain vermiculite before installing any type of central heating or cooling system with the air handler in the attic. Asbestos flooring tiles, old vinyl flooring, and flooring adhesives were common in kitchens and basements for many years. When they are damaged, such as during a renovation, they can release toxic fibers.

Some people suggest leaving asbestos-related materials alone and just going over them. However, later remodeling projects could disturb the material and release the fibers into the air. Extensive water damage could also loosen flooring tiles, leading them to break. When possible, it's best to just remove all asbestos-related materials, but this should be done by a certified asbestos-removal professional, which can be costly. In some locales, an asbestos-removal permit is required, and proper care must be taken to make sure no asbestos fibers are released into the air. Removal should consist of sealing off the work area and using special air filters and vacuums to catch and trap airborne fibers released during the remediation process.

Formaldehyde is another product added to many building materials during the manufacturing process. High levels of formaldehyde are considered dangerous and have been linked to various types of cancers; it is considered a carcinogen. Formaldehyde is especially common in wood products such as flooring, pressed or composite wood, plywood, wood adhesives, and some cabinets. Formaldehyde is considered a volatile organic compound (VOC). Proposition 65 pertains to California residents and requires companies to label products made with high levels of VOCs or other toxic or cancer-causing materials, like formaldehyde. Proposition 65 was passed by California residents in 1986 and is officially known and the Safe Drinking Water and Toxic Enforcement Act of 1986. Many people are turning toward products that are known to be free of formaldehyde.

Green Building

As people have become more aware of how our actions can affect the health of the planet, there has been a growing awareness that we need to take steps to protect our resources and guard against products that are harmful to the environment. Alternative sources of energy, such as solar and wind power, are becoming increasingly popular in some locations, but green building has become a market unto itself in residential home construction, with many companies marketing green products.

Green building is an expansive topic that is too much to cover in detail in this book. There also seem to be differing technical definitions of what green building is as it relates to residential home construction. Generally speaking, green building refers to using materials and systems that are environmentally friendly, meaning they are energy efficient; produce less of a carbon footprint; are sustainable; do not emit VOCs or other by-products that are harmful to people, animals, or the environment; do not affect air quality; and require less energy to create than traditional building products and methods. The use of recycled materials is another main component of green building.

Buying energy-efficient appliances is not a new concept but is considered a form of green building because they consume less energy than other appliances. Look for appliances that have the yellow Energy Star label. The Energy Star program is a joint venture between the US Department of Energy and the US Environmental Protect Agency (Lester and McGuerty 2016, 43).

Other labels and certifications to look for when choosing green building materials are the Leadership in Energy and Environmental Design (LEED) certification and Greenguard. LEED was first developed by the US Green Building Council and is a well-respected green building certification program. Greenguard, originally derived from the Greenguard Environmental Institute, started as an independent organization concerned with testing the indoor air quality of products (Lester and McGuerty 2016, 44). Their certification program focuses on testing materials and products to make sure they emit only low levels of VOCs. Look for the UL Greenguard certification label.

Rooms with southern and western exposures are areas of heat gain because of their exposure to the sun. Blocking the bright sun is a great way to keep a home cool, save energy, and protect materials from the sun's rays, which can cause fading. Often thought of as old fashioned but still seen in many older neighborhoods, window awnings might be the original form of "green cooling" and can add character to a home while helping keep rooms cool. Awnings are typically put up in the spring and removed in the fall to allow for more natural light during the darker winter months. However, year-round awnings are available. Many awning companies service residential properties as well as their commercial clients and can store your awnings for the winter. Awnings block the sun's rays before they enter your windows. Without awnings, thick, room-darkening window treatments are needed to block the sun after its rays pass through the window. When lowered, you can't see out the windows without moving the window treatments. Awnings have the added benefit of allowing you to see out the windows and keep the windows open while still blocking the sun.

In addition to solar energy, geothermal heating and cooling systems are gaining in popularity for new homes but are not suitable as a retrofit for older homes. Geothermal systems use the natural heating and cooling properties of the earth to heat and cool water that is then circulated throughout the house.

In short, there is an array of green building products and techniques that many homeowners are incorporating into their new homes and additions. Some systems are better suited for different climates than others, and the upfront costs of some of the products can be high. Any initial cost should be compared to the energy savings over the life of the home and your time there. Still, many things can be done to make your home more energy efficient and environmentally friendly. Here are a few:

- Use Energy Star–rated appliances.
- Solar energy is gaining in popularity but has limitations in colder climates compared to the Sunbelt states.
- Programmable thermostats can be a great way to conserve energy when you are not home.

- Insulation, especially in older homes, is a great way to increase energy efficiency by keeping warm air from escaping and blocking cold air and heat from the sun from entering.
- Permeable pavers allow water back into the earth and reduce water runoff.
- Install window awnings.
- Replacing old windows or upgrading weather stripping and installing new storm windows can help a great deal.
- Radiant hot-water heating systems are very efficient and reduce the amount of dust and allergens circulated through the house.
- Consider geothermal heating and cooling systems where applicable.
- Use LED light bulbs.
- Reduce or illuminate products with formaldehyde and other VOCs.
- Remove carpeting, which can be a haven for allergens, such as dust and dander.
- Use air filters to purify the indoor air.
- Allow for proper ventilation to keep moisture and humidity levels low and to ward off mold.

It is important to note that many products are marketed as green products simply because they are energy efficient even though they might violate other aspects of accepted green building. An example would be spray foam insulation. Spray foam insulation has gained immense popularity with homeowners and builders the last several years because of its high R-value and ability to get into tiny nooks and crannies and expand, thereby sealing off virtually any space where air loss or infiltration occurs. However, spray foam insulation is a cocktail of toxic chemicals that are mixed, often on site, to create the polyurethane foam. Isocyanates are chemicals such as methylene diphenyl diisocyanate (MDI), which are mixed with polyols that react to form the foam. When not cured properly, meaning not fully reacted, the chemicals can off-gas, or emit orders. The curing process can also produce other chemicals that contain VOCs. The Building Green website has a great article from 2011 (updated in 2018) that details the US Environmental Protection Agency's growing concerns about spray foam insulation, particularly when applied as a do-it-yourself-job (Roberts 2011). Does a product that contains so many chemicals and that has to be applied by a person wearing a safety suit truly sound "green" just because it is energy efficient? See Badore (2018) for alternatives to spray foam insulation and Alter (2019) for other warnings from the Treehugger website.

Liability Insurance

General contractors carry liability insurance, commonly known as builder's risk, to protect them in the event they are sued or property is damaged. They also carry workmen's compensation insurance, which protects them if workers are injured on the job and covers the workers' lost wages and medical care. Subcontractors also carry various types of liability insurance. All contractors should be licensed, bonded, and insured. To be bonded means the insured has obtained a surety bond, which is a promise by the surety company to pay the harmed party if they suffer from harmful or dishonest business practices or if the insured does not fulfill his or her obligations. In this case, liability insurance protects the contractor, and the surety bond protects the homeowner. Bonding is meant to provide an added measure of reassurance and protection to consumers when dealing with certain businesses. If you use a general contractor, make sure you get a copy of their liability and bonding information. Get a copy of their actual certificate of insurance and the name of the surety company. If you act as your own general contractor, you should still get the same information from all your subcontractors in addition to obtaining your own liability insurance that is in force during the life of your project.

Talk to your insurance provider about this, but at the minimum, you should increase the liability insurance on your homeowner's policy. I also strongly recommend that you purchase additional insurance separate from your homeowner's policy to protect you in the event you are sued, someone gets injured on your property, or damage occurs to someone else's property as a result of your construction. Builder's risk insurance typically covers unoccupied structures during construction and doesn't cover personal property. If you are living in your home during your renovation, builder's risk might not apply to your situation, so talk to your insurance agent about increasing your liability protection. In either case, you want to make sure the insurance protects any materials brought to and stored on your property from theft, damage, fire, or "acts of God," as they say in the insurance industry, so you are not out the money if something happens to any materials delivered to your site before they are used. Also, talk to your insurance provider about whether or not you need to obtain any type of workmen's compensation insurance in case a worker gets injured on your job. You might need, or want, this extra measure of protection, even if the subcontractors you hired have workmen's compensation insurance for themselves and their employees. Insurance laws vary from state to state, so make sure to talk to your insurance agent about all your options. In this case, it is definitely better to be safe than sorry.

Chapter 3
Finding and Hiring
Subcontractors

Be practical as well as generous in your ideals. Keep your eyes on the stars, but remember to keep your feet on the ground.

—Theodore Roosevelt

General contractors are not hard to find. You can find many contractors simply by looking for signs at other construction projects, looking in your local paper, searching the internet, and talking to friends and neighbors who have had work done. Word of mouth from people who had a good experience with a contractor can be the best way to find contractors, as well as visiting jobsites where you like the work being done.

It can be more difficult for a homeowner acting as their own general contractor to find all the proper subcontractors for a major renovation, let alone to build an entire house or addition. This is often the biggest challenge a homeowner faces when they want to act as their own general contractor. However, some of the same ideas mentioned above still apply. Additionally, your architect can be a great source of referrals for general contractors and subcontractors. Here are a few other ideas for finding subcontractors:

- Ask for the names of specific types of contractors at building supply stores. These are stores where contractors typically purchase their materials, such as lumberyards, brickyards, drywall suppliers, HVAC and plumbing supply stores, et cetera—not your typical big box home center.
- Many municipalities have a database of licensed tradesmen. This list can contain the names of the various companies and tradesmen licensed to do business in that municipality, like general contractors, plumbing contractors, electrical contractors, masons, et cetera. The Chicago Department of Buildings has a

public database of licensed contractors and subcontractors on its website. Check your municipality for the same type of information.

- Visit jobsites and try to get various subcontractors' information.
- Seek referrals from tradesmen. They often know others in the building trades.
- Check the internet and the Yellow Pages.
- Look for or place classified ads seeking subcontractors.

It is important, when looking for carpenters, to distinguish between framing contractors, interior carpenters, and trim carpenters. Rough framing is an entirely different beast from basic general carpentry. Among other things, rough framing of a new home or addition requires the lifting of heavy beams of wood, working high up, measuring for window and door openings, et cetera. Rough framers often have an entirely different set of skills related to structural framing than basic interior carpenters. Trim carpenters specialize in the more precise and delicate carpentry work after the walls are up, such as installing wood trim, moldings, door and window casings, et cetera. Additionally, rough plumbing can consist of sewer line work and running all the water supply and drain lines. Your local plumber who only repairs sinks and toilets might not be the person for this job unless he has a lot of rough plumbing experience and has other people to help him. Make sure you are hiring the right people for all the specific jobs.

Once you have found some potential contractors, schedule a meeting with them to go over your project and see which ones are interested in working with you and submitting bids for your project. General contractors and subcontractors will usually have their own contracts drawn up and ready to be signed by the homeowner once a proposal is generated and accepted. If anything, you want included in the contract is not there, do not be afraid to ask that it be added. If it is a reasonable request, the contractor should not mind putting it in the contract and agreeing to it in writing. Do not settle for handshake or verbal agreements. Items that are clearly spelled out in writing protect everyone in the event of a misunderstanding, disagreement, or litigation. Do not hire anyone without a contract. Unfortunately, the cost of litigation often far outweighs the loss of money in many smaller situations, but a solid contract protects you in the event you have to sue someone or take them to small claims court.

Also, if any subcontractors have to return to finish their job after other trades have finished their part, considering withholding a portion of the final payment (10 percent is recommended) to ensure the subcontractors return when needed. Be sure to write this into the contract. Examples of this might include a masonry contractor who has to return at a later date to cut through to the existing house on an addition if it is not done right away, a framing carpenter who might have to return to frame out the openings of a cut-through, a roofer who might have to return to install flashing around plumbing and exhaust vents that were not previously installed, and concrete contractors who have to return to pour the driveway and sidewalks after all other work is completed.

Do not try to reinvent the wheel by spending your time and money drawing up all your own contracts. Find sample contracts for the various trades online if you like, but generally speaking, it does not matter whose contract you use as long as everything you expect is clearly covered. Ask the subcontractor to include items you discussed in the contract they create. Here are some things to keep in mind when hiring general contractors and subcontractors:

- Look for reviews from the Better Business Bureau or on websites such as Angie's List or do an internet search to see what you can learn.
- Make sure your contractors are licensed, bonded, and insured.
- Ask how big a crew they have and how long the work is expected to take. Make sure their time frame is written into the contract. Delays can cost you time and money, especially if the next crew cannot get in to start the next phase of work until the previous crew is done.
- Consider adding a penalty clause with a per diem amount if the work takes far longer than expected because they underestimated the scope of the project or workers are not showing up.
- Make sure your subcontractors will be on the job every day when possible. Bad weather and delays in obtaining materials that are not available are valid reasons for workers not showing up, but make sure you are not a side job the contractors get to when they can. If so, you should be paying them a lot less for the job.
- Ask for referrals from previous customers.
- Ask to see photos of previous projects.
- Request a copy of their insurance liability or builder's risk policy.

- Only work with contractors who will provide a written contract that outlines the scope of their work and includes all the details of the work to be performed.
- Make sure your general contractor and subcontractors warranty their work. You should get the manufacturer's warranty on any product they install, and the contractor should cover the labor cost to repair anything for at least a year. Make sure your contractors are installing products in line with the recommendations of the manufacturer; otherwise, the manufacturer's warranty could be voided.
- Make sure your contract spells out the cost of any work not included in the contract that might arise or that you might want to add. For example, if the contractor charges $75 per hour per man for additional work, make sure this is spelled out in the contract, or draw up a separate contract for the extra work, such as framing a new basement, that you were originally not going to do.
- Find out if your contractor or subcontractor charges a fee for change orders. There should be no cost or very little cost to make changes to work that has not been completed yet unless an architect has to sign off on it, a new permit is needed, new materials have to be ordered, other materials cannot be returned, or certain work has to be redone to accommodate the changes. Be aware that some changes can affect the entire structure, so be reasonable about what you want changed.
- Make sure all changes are agreed to in writing, especially changes not on the original blueprints. Draw up a change order form that includes the date and any costs involved if your contractor does not have one. This way, no one can say they did not know about the changes you wanted or what it would cost.
- Make sure your contract covers every aspect of each subcontractor's job and the expectations of all parties.
- Make sure your contracts spell out deposits and payments. Usually, payments are made to general contractors and subcontractors as different phases of the project are completed. For example, a rough framing contractor might require an initial deposit, a second payment when the basic framing is complete, a third payment when the roof framing is complete, and final payment when all other work is done.

- Make sure your contract stipulates what forms of payment are acceptable: personal check, money order, cashier's check, credit card payment, bank draft, cash, et cetera.
- Make sure your contract stipulates who pays for the materials and delivery.
- To use your subcontractor's discount for materials, they might have to be the one to order the materials, then be reimbursed by you unless you can pay the supplier directly. Make sure these terms are spelled out in writing.
- Make sure all contractors clean up and dispose of their waste. Find out if disposal for anything they might have to haul away is included in their fee.
- If a dumpster is required, find out if that is part of the contractor's fee. If so, and you are providing the dumpsters, deduct this cost from their fee. Get the biggest dumpster you can, usually thirty cubic yards.
- If you are working with a general contractor, the finished product should be move-in ready or, as they say in real estate closings, in "broom-clean" condition. Make sure this is specified in the contract.
- Do not make a final payment until all work is done to your satisfaction.
- Always obtain lien waivers and a sworn statement from your contractors to protect yourself against mechanics' liens.

Builder Alert: Your contractors must install products in line with the recommendations of the manufacturer; otherwise, the manufacturer's warranty could be voided.

If a contractor is hesitant to put any reasonable requests into writing without a good reason, it might be a red flag and cause for concern. If contractors are not getting back to you with answers to your questions, not keeping their scheduled appointments with you, or not getting bids to you in a timely manner, it might be a good idea to pass on them. Contractors are busy, but if they are too busy to respond to potential clients or show up when they are supposed to, especially without a cancellation notice and a good reason, then you probably do not want them working on your project. The way a person runs their business is usually a reflection of their work ethic and how they do their job. Too many red flags before a job has even started does not bode well for the project once it starts. For this reason, I do not recommend paying someone a deposit before work has started. If a contractor wants a deposit, tell them they will get it when the work starts. I say this from experience because I hired people for a job who simply never showed up. Whether they did not really want the job; got too busy with their other projects; or were making more money on bigger, more lucrative jobs, it does not matter. They made a commitment and broke it, and if I had given them a deposit ahead of time, I probably would have been out the money without litigation, as well as having to find another contractor. Also, many banks will not fund construction loans if the general contractor requires a deposit.

Lastly, but most perhaps most important, always obtain lien waivers from your general contractor or all your subcontractors if you are acting as your own general contractor. If a contractor is not paid, they can put a lien on your house, known as a mechanic's lien. Most people will not even know this was done until a title search is performed when they go to refinance or sell their home. If you pay a general contractor for a job, you assume he paid all his subcontractors for the work they did, but that is not always the case, especially if the contractor is having financial difficulty. If they skip out on paying their subcontractors, you might not know it, but the subcontractors can still put a lien on your house. If you get into a dispute with a subcontractor and they claim you did not pay them, they can put a mechanic's lien on your home.

Many states have mechanic's lien acts that require general contractors to provide you with a signed and notarized list of the people and companies they hired, along with the amounts owed to each party after payment is made. This is called a sworn statement, and you should request one from your general contractor before any final payments are made. If your state does not have official sworn statement or final waiver of lien forms you can download, then check with an attorney or your local title company.

> **Builder Alert: Always obtain lien waivers and a sworn statement from your contractors to protect yourself against mechanic's liens.**

Chapter 4
Estimating Prices

I do know that when I am 60, I should be attempting to achieve different personal goals than those which had priority at age 20.

—Warren Buffett

Once a contractor or supplier has the blueprints for your project, they will perform what is known as a takeoff. This means they will go over every aspect of the drawings to arrive at certain prices to do the job. Though the words are used interchangeably, there is a technical difference between bids and estimates. An estimate is a general idea of what a project might cost. Bids are proposals from contractors to do a certain job for a certain amount of money. Estimates are lists of numbers contractors and homeowners can put together comprising the cost of labor and materials. Bids are written proposals and outline the scope of work to be performed. Bids are always preferable to general estimates, and contractors will usually include the cost of materials in their bids. This can save you, acting as the contractor, a lot of time, but it is still good to have a general idea of what things cost to make sure you are not overcharged. Subcontractors typically do not mark up their materials prices like a general contractor might, but they often get contractor discounts from supply houses that the general public does not get.

General contractors might be able to bid on a project using the knowledge and experience they already have and base their prices on square footage, similar projects, or other formulas. There are even builder takeoff software programs and cost-estimating guides some general contractors use. However, the more details unique to your project that are included, the more accurate contractors can be in the bidding process.

Many times, general contractors will give the blueprints to the various subcontractors they use for bids on individual aspects of the project, such as the rough framing contractor, the plumbing contractor, the roofing contractor, the HVAC contractor, the excavation contractor, the concrete contractor, et cetera. They might even submit the blueprints to a lumber supply house and brick company for materials prices. This process could take a few weeks, depending on how busy the various parties are involved in the process. Use the form at the end of this chapter to put together a rough estimate of your project or give it to general contractors when asking for bids. Make your own spreadsheet using Microsoft Excel to help you with a detailed budget.

If you are acting as your own general contractor, then it is up to you to meet with all the subcontractors; explain the scope of the project; give them the blueprints; and explain any special or unusual obstacles, requirements, or requests for the project. See if the architect is available to attend the first meeting with the subcontractors to go over the details of the project. Be honest and upfront about the scope of the work to be performed. Don't try to hide any extra or unusual work you want done. This will only lead to problems down the road if the subcontractor wants more money for additional work that was not in the original contract.

You also want to make sure the contractor can perform all the required work. If something is not within the subcontractor's field of expertise, everyone needs to know this upfront. Any bids for labor and materials you receive will likely have an expiration date, after which the bid is no longer valid. There is a legitimate reason for this beyond the contractor wanting a commitment from you. Material and labor costs vary greatly from location to location, and costs can change over time because of things like supply and demand, tariffs, and other factors that affect the prices of materials and commodities. The cost of things like lumber, steel, copper piping, and other building materials can change over the course of a couple of months. This can add up to a great deal of money when ordering materials for an entire house or a large addition. Industry standards also dictate ordering 10 percent more materials than needed for waste and mistakes that are likely to occur so that you or your contractor do not have to constantly order more materials or pay extra delivery fees for small orders.

When contractors are busy with a lot of work, they can afford to say no to projects they do not really want to spend their time on or that might not be as profitable. They can also charge higher rates because their demand is high. If business is slow, contractors are often willing to cut their prices just to get some work. Therefore, be aware of the external factors that might be affecting the estimates you get and understand that if you wait six months or a year to start the project, your costs could change drastically in that time. For all these reasons, I have found that websites that help people estimate the cost of a project based on their zip codes and information input about their projects are not very helpful or accurate. In the end, the only estimates that matter are the bids you get for materials and labor for your specific job, in your specific location, at a specific time, and from the contractors or subcontractors who might actually do the work.

The number one job of the homeowner is to make sure they are not getting overcharged by a general contractor. When acting as their own general contractor, the main job of the homeowner is to get accurate estimates for materials and labor from each of the subcontractors. Not only is this vital to managing a budget, but accurate estimates will also be needed when it comes time to finance and pay for your project.

Eliminating the middleman, the general contractor, and hiring all the subcontractors is the number-one way a homeowner can save a fortune on a major construction project. This puts the responsibility on the homeowner to research the prevailing market conditions in their area for materials and labor. The only way to do this is to get estimates from building supply houses for materials and from subcontractors for their labor. Use the internet or phone directory to locate building supply houses in your area. Even if you are using a general contractor, you can use your estimates to make sure you are getting a fair price. Show your estimates to your general contractor and use them to negotiate. Do not be afraid to ask your general contractor if you can use your own subcontractors. Try to get at least three different estimates from general contractors, all your subcontractors, and building supply houses. As mentioned previously, a number of factors can affect prices, but getting three estimates for most aspects of the project provides a good benchmark of what things will likely cost. You might also be surprised at how prices can vary from one contractor to another.

Builder Alert: Always try to get three estimates for materials and labor for each aspect of the project.

Start with taking your blueprints to various lumber supply houses and requesting a takeoff of all the lumber that will be needed. Reputable lumber houses do this all the time and often even accept electronic versions of the blueprints submitted via email or uploaded to their websites. It might take a couple of weeks, depending how busy they are, but they will be able to provide you with an itemized list of every piece of lumber and plywood needed for the job. A building supply house might also be able to supply the roofing material, insulation, siding, windows, doors, and a host of other products and ask you if you want those items included in your estimate. This will require checking out all their other building products. Be aware that their other items might be stock or builder-grade items, rather than custom products. If you know you will be getting your windows and doors from another supplier, you have a roofer lined up, and you will be using a separate company for insulation, do not bother with the extras and just stick to the lumber estimate. Ask if they give discounts to contractors that you can qualify for (you are acting as your own contractor) or if you can receive the discount if your subcontractor places the order. Get a separate price for nails, screws, glue, anchor bolts, joist hangers, and any other materials that might be needed for the job. Once you get your bid for the lumber, you have an idea of what the materials will cost regardless of the subcontractor you hire for the framing. Compare this price to the cost the rough framing contractor gives you if he were to order all the materials.

The same lumber supply house should be able to give you a price on all the door and window trim and other wood moldings based on the linear footage needed. This can be just a rough estimate as I found it best to have a trim carpenter measure everything and tell me exactly what to order when it came to that phase of the project (more about this in Chapter 18). I was even able to submit my blueprints online to the insulation company and get a quote for the job that way. Repeat the process with a brick supplier (you might have to meet with the representative from the brickyard to choose a brick style and color and any limestone sills, thresholds, or accents you want) and a drywall supplier. These will be the largest quantities of materials you will need to purchase. You can also estimate the cost of copper and cast-iron piping per liner foot and the cost of roofing materials from respective supply houses, but the subcontractors will most likely order what they need themselves or tell you exactly what to order. Always make sure you get the receipts, but be aware the receipts do not always reflect any builder discounts your subcontractors might get, so be sure to ask about that. The HVAC contractor will likely order everything they need themselves. The best way to control your costs is to order everything yourself, get the materials delivered to your site, and see if you can get your subcontractors' discounts.

Flooring and Tile

Estimate the square footage of flooring and wall covering you will need for backsplashes, bathroom floors, showers, et cetera. Visit flooring and tile stores to get an idea of what different materials and installation cost. Nowadays, it seems as if many retail flooring places only sell and install prefinished wood floors. If you are interested in wood floors that you want stained a custom color—for example, if you are trying to match an existing wood floor—find a wholesale flooring store and a floor installer/refinisher. You will need this person for the job anyway, so ask where they buy their materials. To tile our kitchen backsplash, I received one estimate for $1,200 and one for $1,500 for labor only. I was able to get the marble tile we wanted plus installation for a total of $1,700 from a local tile store. This was a huge savings, so it definitely pays to shop around and seek multiple estimates. Make sure your estimates include grout, underlayment, spacers, water barriers, sealers, and whatever ancillary materials your job might require. Dedicated tile stores are usually aware of all the necessary materials and will factor them into your quote.

Doors and Windows

If you want quality or custom doors and windows, visit a showroom that specializes in these products rather than buying "builder grade" from building supply houses. Many people spend hundreds of thousands of dollars on a new home only to have extremely low-quality hollow-core doors installed inside the house by the builder. You can buy these doors for $60 at most home centers, and it is easy to accidentally put holes in them. Shop around for quality interior wood doors; they are more durable, look better, and block sound better. Mill shops can also custom make doors, which is great if you are trying to match existing doors for an addition. This can be expensive, but it's a worthwhile option, depending on your design and taste.

Windows are a main architectural feature of a home and also serve important functional and aesthetic purposes. There are many different types, styles, and designs of windows. Work closely with your architect and window representative to choose windows that fit the character of your home and the lighting, view, and airflow needs of each room in the house. Don't skimp on windows just to save some money. Quality windows cost more for a reason. You want windows that look good but will also last a long time and protect your home from unwanted drafts, noise, and water penetration.

If you are trying to match the style, size, or muntin design (the dividers that separate panes of glass in a window) of the new windows for your addition to the existing windows of your home, you will probably need custom windows. You can also locate and visit showrooms that offer windows and doors direct from the manufacturer. This is where you or your contractors can receive a builder discount. Pella, Marvin, and Anderson are among the best and most reputable and also offer windows in a variety of styles, materials, and finishes. I purchased our windows from a Pella showroom and received a contractor discount by having my rough framing carpenter purchase them using his account.

In the last few decades, windows have improved drastically over the single-pane windows of the past and offer improved benefits when it comes to protection from heat loss. Quality new windows can protect your home from heat loss, ultraviolet light, and drafts, making your home more energy efficient and cutting your heating costs. Double-pane and thermal-pane windows contain multiple layers of glass to reduce heat transfer between your home and the outside. They can also contain an insulating layer of gas, usually argon, between the panes of glass, which makes them even more effective. Low-emissivity (Low-E) glass protects your home from infrared and ultraviolet light. This reduces your energy costs and also protects your home from the harmful effects of UV rays, which can damage (fade) your furniture, flooring, carpeting, and window treatments.

If you are building a new home or addition, the size of the windows will be based on the rough openings. It is best to let your carpenter or window representative take the measurements, so if there are any mistakes, they are responsible. Many of these showrooms sell entry doors as well. Interior doors come in a variety of styles and materials, and the costs vary. Figure out how many doors you need and start shopping around. I wanted the interior doors of our addition to match the 1920s-era single-panel doors in the existing house. One general contractor quoted me a price of $9,000 to replicate four of these doors. I kept visiting a salvage house in Chicago, and sure enough, I finally hit the jackpot with their recent cache and found six interior doors that were an exact match to our existing doors. I bought those six doors plus other doors I liked for a total of $750, which included delivery. The varying sizes did not matter since the new framing could be built to suit the various doors. I didn't even have to paint or refinish some of the doors; otherwise, sanding, painting, or refinishing could produce doors that look like new if they are in relatively good shape. I hit the jackpot at the salvage store, but interior doors can still be custom milled.

In the case of windows and doors, and all interior wood trim for that matter, decide if you will be painting them or staining them. If you want to stain them, you will need to purchase windows, doors, and trim that come in a quality stain-grain wood, such as oak, maple, or birch. Pine is a harder, less porous wood that does not take stain well. Rather than absorb the stain, pine and other low-quality materials, such as medium-density fiberboard (MDF), which has no grain to it, keep stain from seeping into the wood, which is how stained wood achieves its deep, rich look. Those materials are better suited for painting.

Storm Windows

If you live in an older home, a major source of heat loss and drafts are old windows. Old single-pane windows are not that effective in keeping cold air out and blocking warm inside air from escaping. This leads to turning up the heat on cold days to compensate for the heat loss. As previously mentioned, there are many options for new windows to improve the comfort and efficiency of your home. However, replacing several old windows in a home is a costly endeavor and one that might not reap rewards when comparing the upfront cost of replacing the windows to the amount of money saved on heating bills. It could take years to recoup the upfront cost of thousands of dollars for new windows. There can also be some destruction involved in replacing old windows as the window casings and framing will have to be removed to get the old windows out. If not done delicately, the casings can be damaged, and it might not be possible to replace them without some custom, and costly, millwork.

Another possibility is to leave the interior windows alone and install new storm windows on the outside for a fraction of the cost. Old-fashioned wood storms are still the best. Wood is an insulator, not a conductor like metal, making it superior to aluminum for storm windows. The wood does not transfer cold from the outside to the inside like metal (think of pots with aluminum handles that get hot on the stove compared to pots with wood handles that do not transfer the heat to your hand). Wood windows also block more sound and do not rattle as much as aluminum, but they have to be custom milled and require painting and maintenance. However, wood storms are definitely preferable when trying to maintain the historic or architectural look of a home. Some millwork companies are now offering wood storm windows with built-in screens so the storm glass can be removed from the inside.

Aluminum storm windows are another option that has come a long way in style and function from the old aluminum storms of decades past. They now come in a variety of colors, are maintenance-free, and come in double- and triple-track options that easily allow a built-in screen to be opened from the inside. Double-track windows have a narrower profile and do not protrude from the opening as much, making them more pleasing aesthetically. They also allow the panels to fold in for cleaning and work well to seal the perimeter of the windows to block drafts (Franco and Vila, n.d.). They also come with some of the features of new windows, such as Low-E glass. In terms of efficiency, some people contend that good exterior storm windows work just as well as brand new windows because the pocket of air between the interior window and exterior storm window acts as an insulating barrier against cold air (Harvey Building Products 2018). In fact, a National Trust for Historic Preservation study (2016) cited the efficacy of installing storm windows compared to new windows. Other studies include Turrell (2000) and Yagid (n.d.).

Old wood windows can be repaired; even the old ropes that go into the framing of the window and are attached to a counterweight to hold the window open can be repaired. Custom millwork companies are getting harder to find, but they can make or replicate doors, window sashes (the part of the window that goes up and down), and woodwork to match what is already in the home if you are preservation minded and want to maintain consistency in the look throughout a home, even after building an addition.

Storm Doors

Storm doors have also come a long way in recent years, in terms of both design and function. Storm doors can protect your main door from the weather and also serve as a second layer of defense against cold air while allowing fresh air inside when it is nice out. Some brands offer in-door storage of a glass panel that lowers to reveal a screen for half the door. This makes it unnecessary to remove the entire storm glass and store it. Aluminum storm doors come in many custom sizes, and the cost can vary from a few hundred dollars to very pricey. Wood storm doors can be custom made by a mill shop. However, one of the most important factors with installing glass storm doors is never to put a storm door over a wood door that is in direct line with the sun's rays, usually on south and west exposures. The heat from the sun's rays gets trapped between the storm door and the wood door, creating an oven-like effect. The trapped heat can cause the wood door to warp and crack. Doing this can void the manufacturer's warranty of new wood doors. In fact, some manufacturers of wood doors specify an awning or other overhang must protrude over the door enough to block the sun's rays. The installation instructions detail the size and protrusion from the house, and not following them will void the door's warranty. Some screen doors have vents at the bottom to release the trapped hot air, but generally speaking, it is best just not to place storm doors over a wood door in direct view of the sun. You can also remove the storm glass if you want to be sure your wood door will not be damaged. The self-storing storm doors that lower the storm window out of the way are another good option because they allow more hot air to escape than storm doors with just vents at the bottom.

> **Builder Alert: Never install a glass storm door over a wood door that is in the direct line of the sun's rays. The heat can crack and warp the wood door and void the manufacturer's warranty.**

Structural Steel

If you need steel beams and lintels for your project, they will be installed by your concrete, masonry, or rough framing contractors. If you are removing a load-bearing wall inside, your carpentry crew will install the new beam. If you require any steel beams as specified by your architect, you will have to order them unless your subcontractors can get them. You can buy lintels that support the openings over windows and doors from a brick supplier, but your subcontractor should be able to procure these. You will have to order large structural beams from a steel supplier, and they might have to be custom made according to the specifications of your architect, especially if they need to be curved or angled. Surprisingly, the steel is not that expensive. For our addition, all the steel beams, the angle irons, and the arched beam over the garage door cost just under $2,000. Make sure your steel company can deliver to your site, and, most importantly, see if their truck has a crane to remove the steel and/or put it into place. If not, the contractor who is installing the steel will have to be there for the delivery and have the machinery to unload the steel and hoist it into place using a crane, a hoist, or jacks. My masonry crew was able to use a forklift to remove the beams and position them using several men on scaffolds. Otherwise, they would have had to rent the proper equipment to hoist the beams into place, which would have added to the cost.

> **Builder Alert: Make sure your crew has the means to move and hoist into place any steel beams that are delivered.**

Kitchens and Baths

Kitchens and baths reap the most rewards in terms of use and resale value of homes. Estimating the price of a new or renovated bathroom is relatively simple. Estimate the cost of the fixtures, such as the sink, toilet, and faucets; the flooring and wall tile; the shower doors; the bathtub; any ancillary products, such as a towel warmer, vents, steam generator, et cetera; and the labor for the plumber, tile installer, painter, and electrician, if needed. In the case of a major renovation, also include the cost of drywall and the cement board needed behind tiled walls. If the bathroom or bathrooms are part of an addition or new home, the cement board cost will be included in the drywall estimate for the entire new structure. The final cost of a new bathroom can vary dramatically, depending on the size of the bathroom, the cost of the materials, and the amenities. Steam showers require a lot of extra prep work, including plumbing, electrical, and a moisture barrier behind the tile, in addition to the cost of the steam generator. (I have included information about installing a steam shower in Chapter 20.) Still, most of these costs can be estimated through some online shopping and talking to the representative at the tile store.

Kitchens are an entity unto themselves. If you are working with an architect, they will most likely just design the general layout of the kitchen and the placement of appliances. You will need to work out the details with a kitchen designer, and the cost can vary dramatically, depending on the type of cabinets, countertops, and appliances you choose. Designing a kitchen requires a lot of time. Most kitchen designers, home centers, and big box stores offer complimentary design assistance, though some might charge a fee that is applied to the cost of the cabinets if you use their services. It is best to shop around a bit to get an idea of what you like and the potential cost of various cabinets before scheduling a design appointment. A kitchen design appointment could take several hours, given all the options and details, and you do not want to do this any more times than necessary. You do not want to waste your time or anyone else's having a kitchen designed by a place you are not going to do busines with in the end. It is just too time consuming.

Cabinets are usually priced per linear foot, as are laminate countertops. The price per linear foot of cabinets can vary dramatically, so have a budget in mind when shopping for them. The cost of granite and quartz countertops is usually based on square footage and whether or not you want a backsplash included. Features such as pull-out shelves, soft-close hardware, pot-and-pan organizers, moldings, glass doors, or other built-in features will increase the cost but will also create a nice kitchen. Use the internet and kitchen-design magazines along with displays at various home centers to get an idea of what you might like and see if you can get a ballpark estimate.

When you are ready for a kitchen design and detailed estimate, narrow down your choices to one or two places and take them your blueprints or measurements of the kitchen. They can save your design for when you are ready for your cabinets, and you will more than likely make changes to your original design. Also find out what their installation price is and compare that to the quote you get from your carpenter. Using an installer who works with the cabinet store can make life a lot easier, even if the installation price is higher than that of your regular carpenter. It is best to use someone who is experienced in installing cabinets so that any mistakes that are made become the responsibility of the cabinet store. It is also easier to have someone knowledgeable about the company and your order to serve as the middleman in case mistakes were made making your cabinets or items are missing.

I found that dedicated granite and marble dealers often have better prices for countertops than the prices quoted by home centers, which often use a separate company for their countertops anyway. However, if you are financing your cabinets through the home center, you can include the cost of your countertops. If you go through a granite or marble company, you might not be able to finance your countertops. If you are using a home equity loan or construction loan to finance your project, it might not matter unless you want to pay for your kitchen separately.

It should be noted that marble showers and countertops look beautiful, but marble is a very porous material that absorbs moisture and therefore stains easily. For this reason, marble is not recommended for countertops or steam showers. Anywhere marble is used, it should be sealed with a marble or stone sealer. Furthermore, steams showers need to have a waterproof barrier, such as Hydro Ban, by Laticrete, installed under the tile to protect the wood studs and other materials from moisture penetration. Steam showers should also use epoxy grout.

Appliances and Lighting

As with cabinets and countertops, the cost of appliances and light fixtures vary dramatically. You can buy a stove for $1,200, or you can pay over $9,000 for a professional-grade Viking-style stove. You can spend $75 or $1,000 on a ceiling fan. Your design tastes, needs, wants, and budget will determine the cost of many items that go into your home. Shop around and provide yourself with a general allowance for appliances and lighting.

Next Steps

When working with a general contractor, they might have "general conditions" as a line item built into their bid; this can include such things as keeping the site clean and safe, storing materials, dumpsters, administrative expenses, insurance cost, et cetera. General conditions are a great place to negotiate for a lower price. Find out from your general contractor exactly what this includes as you do not want to be charged for things twice or pay for a contractor's normal cost of doing business. If you are paying for the permits or dumpsters yourself, for example, your contractor should not be charging you for them. If you are contracting the project yourself, use this line item to set aside money for items such as liability insurance, a cleaning crew, a crew to help you move household items around, or simple demolition during the construction of an addition.

Once you have your basic materials quoted, it's time to meet with general contractors or subcontractors to get bids for all the major work that needs to be performed. Use the list on the next page to keep track of the subcontractors and the work needed to complete your project. If you are considering using a general contractor, duplicate this list for them and ask for a breakdown of expenses. The list can be used for an addition or a new home. The list is more for estimating the labor and materials needed to build your structure, not the specifics of kitchens and bathrooms. Costs for kitchens and baths can vary dramatically. Most general contractors include an allowance for kitchens—say, between $10,000 and $15,000—knowing the final cost might be more or less, depending on what the homeowner wants.

Schedule appointments with the various subcontractors needed for your project, give them a copy of the blueprints, and explain in detail everything that has to be done or that you want or expect from the job. See if your architect can attend the meetings in case there are any specific questions that need to be answered. Make sure to have them separate the labor from the materials cost, and find out if they receive any builder discounts from their supply houses. Also, do not forget to ask if they can discount their price for accepting cash payments. In any case, always get receipts for every payment you make, and do not do business with anyone who will not provide a signed contract outlining the scope of their work. It might take a few weeks to receive bids back from each contractor, but when possible, make sure to get estimates from at least three different contractors for each type of work involved.

Project Estimate Worksheet

1. Survey $_____
2. Architect fees $_____
3. Permits $_____
4. Dumpster $_____
5. Construction fencing $_____
6. Porta potty rental $_____
7. Move or connect utilities $_____
8. Excavation $_____
9. Concrete (foundation and driveway) $_____
10. Masonry or siding $_____
11. Structural steel $_____
12. Rough framing and house wrap $_____
13. Roof (facia, soffit, and gutters) $_____
14. HVAC $_____
15. Plumbing and sewer connection $_____
16. Electrical $_____
17. Insulation $_____
18. Windows and doors $_____
19. Garage doors $_____
20. Window and door hardware $_____
21. Drywall/plaster work $_____
22. Trim carpentry $_____
23. Wood flooring $_____
24. Tile flooring $_____
25. Lighting allowance $_____
26. Kitchen cabinet allowance $_____
27. Installation of cabinets $_____
28. Countertops $_____
29. Kitchen backsplash tile $_____
30. Appliance allowance $_____
31. Bathroom fixtures $_____
32. Bathroom wall tile $_____
33. Painting $_____
34. Landscaping $_____
35. General conditions $_____
36. Overhead and profit $_____
     Total $_____

Chapter 5
Financing Your Project

You measure the size of the accomplishment by the
obstacles you have to overcome to reach your goals.
—Booker T. Washington

Financing the construction of your new home or addition is obviously one of the most critical aspects of your project. Unless you have a large amount of cash, you will likely have to obtain some type of financing. Many lenders do not finance the sale of land by itself. Some lenders might require a 50 percent down payment on land sales. If you are building a home on a lot being sold through a developer, typically in a new subdivision, the lot will be wrapped into the construction loan. However, if you are purchasing land with plans to build on it at a later date, your lender might not finance the sale of the lot. In a regular mortgage, the home acts as collateral for the loan; if the borrower defaults on the loan, the lender still has the home to sell, which can offset the loss. However, the value of unimproved land varies widely, and if a borrower is going to default on a loan, it will probably be on the lot loan rather than a mortgage on their current home. For these reasons, lot loans are considered risky, and many lenders do not offer them. Therefore, if you plan to purchase a lot for investment purposes or to build on at a later date, check around to see what lenders offer lot loans and under what terms.

Though it is becoming more common, in the past, some lenders were also reluctant to give construction loans to homeowners acting as their own general contractors because they were worried about cost overruns that could affect the final loan amount. While this is no longer an issue with some lending institutions, it is still a good idea to shop around and make sure the lender you want to work with will give you a construction loan if you are not using a licensed general contractor. If you are building a new home, you also have to know if you can afford to start your construction project while living in your current home or if you will have to sell your current home first or possibly obtain a bridge loan that will allow you to start construction and sell your current home at a later time.

Everyone's situation is different, so it is best to consult with a loan officer from the start to see what options are available and what makes the most sense, given your financial and living situations. You can also make use of online and smartphone apps that have mortgage and amortization calculators to estimate what various loan amounts will cost on a monthly basis. You can even experiment with the numbers to see how putting extra money toward the principal each month can save a fortune in interest and allow you to pay off the loan faster. Do not forget to include property taxes and insurance in your monthly payments.

Debt-to-Income Ratio

Many people have to take out a construction, home equity, or bridge loan to finance their project. The specific criteria needed to close these loans might depend on the type of loan and the specific project, but the financial requirements to qualify for these loans are similar to those for a regular mortgage, in that the ability to repay the new loan has to be supported by the homeowner's income and creditworthiness and an appraisal of the property. Lenders use debt-to-income ratios (DTI) to determine if a borrower makes enough money to afford the loan. The lower the DTI, the less risk associated with giving someone a loan, so the more likely that person is to be approved. Only debt obligation payments are used in this formula, such as housing payments, car payments, credit card payments, school loans, child support, alimony, and other types of debt that show up on a credit score. Monthly expenses like groceries, utilities, gasoline, savings, retirement investments, insurance payments, spending money, et cetera, which are also part of a normal household budget, do not factor into debt-to-income ratios but are still very important when a borrower is trying to decide how much they can afford. There are various debt-to-income calculators you can experiment with online; however, DTI guidelines can vary from lender to lender and can be affected by the size, purpose, and type of loan.

Many lenders prefer a 28 percent front-end DTI ratio (housing-related expenses such as mortgage, property taxes, and homeowner's insurance) with a back-end DTI ratio (all other monthly debts) of 36 percent, but some lenders will go higher, and other items, such as credit score, savings, and the type of loan are important factors that can affect the DTI lenders will accept. It is best to consult a loan officer, and it's a good idea to hold off on any major purchases, such as buying a new car, until after you close on your loan.

Property Taxes

All municipal taxing bodies calculate their property taxes differently, but the final property tax bill is always based to some degree on the assessed value of the property as determined by the municipal county assessor's office. Additionally, it is important to remember that property taxes are escrowed, or set aside, by the mortgage company and paid to the taxing body by the bank. The mortgage company adds the prorated cost of the yearly taxes to the monthly mortgage payment. Since property taxes are factored into the debt-to-income ratio, high property taxes can affect whether a borrower qualifies for a loan if the DTI is tight. Furthermore, unimproved land is always taxed at a lower rate than land with a home.

Property taxes are also often paid in arrears, depending on the taxing body. That means when you pay your taxes, you are actually paying the taxes for the previous year. Please keep this in mind when building a new home on a vacant lot or in a new subdivision. Homeowners have often been stunned by how much their property taxes increase a couple of years after they first bought the land and started building. After your home is built, you will be taxed not on a vacant lot but on improved land with a home potentially worth several hundred thousand dollars, dramatically increasing your property tax bill. It is not uncommon for people to build a new home, then not be able to afford it after the property taxes shoot up. Even putting an addition on your home can increase your property taxes once the home is reassessed. Therefore, the cost of future taxes should be considered when thinking about how much you can afford to spend on a home or addition.

Credit Score

Your credit score is also a major factor in determining whether you will qualify for a loan and the interest rate charged. Your credit score is a determination of your likelihood to repay the loan based on your credit history or your history of paying off loans and making monthly payments in a timely manner. Too much debt, debt too close to your credit limits, too many late payments, or debt that lingers unpaid for too long can all adversely affect your credit score. You do not need a top credit score to qualify for a loan, but people with better credit pay lower interest rates. A high interest rate from a low credit score can also prevent you from getting a loan if your debt-to-income ratio is tight because a high interest rate means a higher monthly payment.

There are three nationwide credit-scoring bureaus lenders consult when running a credit check—Equifax, Experian, and TransUnion. Not all creditors report to all three bureaus, so lenders often use a blended score. The breakdown of credit scores is usually as follows:

Excellent	800–850
Very Good	740–799
Good	670–739
Fair	580–669
Poor	300–579

Appraisals

A real estate appraisal is required for all residential mortgages. It assures the bank that the property is worth enough money to serve as collateral for a loan. Appraisals are calculated by comparing the subject property to similar homes in the area (comparable properties) and making adjustments in price for factors that affect the subject property when compared to the other properties. For example, if all the homes your house is compared to have two-car garages and your home only has a one-car garage, the appraiser will deduct money from the value of your home when doing the comparison. If your home has four bedrooms, a new kitchen, and updated bathrooms, the appraiser will raise the value of your home to reflect the extra bedroom and the other improvements compared to homes with fewer bedrooms and no updates.

Banks typically seek an 80 percent loan-to-value ratio (LTV), meaning they usually will only lend the borrower up to 80 percent of the value of a home. That means the borrower has to come up with a 20 percent down payment. For example, if a borrower wants to buy a $100,000 home appraised at $100,000, they have to come up with $20,000 in cash because the bank will only lend them 80 percent of the appraised value. Certain types of government-sponsored loan programs, such as the FHA (Federal Housing Administration) and the VA (Department of Veterans Affairs), offer lower down payment options. Other conventional loans requiring less than 20 percent down require the homeowner to purchase private mortgage insurance (PMI), which is added to the cost of the mortgage, along with the property taxes and insurance.

If a home does not appraise at the needed amount, the borrower will have to make up the difference in cash or be turned down for the loan. Using our previous example, what if the home's appraised value is $75,000? The bank will only lend 80 percent of that $75,000 appraised value, or $60,000. Now the borrower has to come up with $40,000 in cash to qualify for the loan and complete the purchase. The home's appraised value after construction is complete is an extremely important consideration when building a new home or addition. If your local real estate market will not bear the cost of a million-dollar home, you might not be able to refinance your construction or home equity loan. In fact, you might not qualify for the construction loan in the first place. Appraisals are market driven, meaning that homes are valued according to what similar homes in the same real estate market sell for at a given time. If the average cost of a home in your area is $350,000 and you just spent $700,000 to build a new home, you might be in trouble when you go to sell or refinance it because your local real estate market might not bear the cost of a $700,000 home. It might not appraise out for a loan you or someone else wants to take out on the property.

This is important whether you use a construction loan or a home equity loan to finance your construction project because you will refinance that loan into a standard conventional loan once your project is complete. In fact, construction loans are based on the perceived value of the home after the project is complete. If the bank does not think the appraised value of your home will be high enough once it is built, you probably will not get the loan. For this reason, it is important to prioritize your spending and make sure you put your money into projects that will likely increase the resale value of the house. Kitchens, baths, and bedrooms are some of the most important factors in determining the value of a home because those are important to most buyers. You don't want to spend $200,000 on an addition and find out it only increased the value of your home by $100,000. Do not put high-end $50,0000 cabinets into a $300,000 house; save those for a $1,000,000 house. You don't want to put more money into a home than you are going to get out of it unless you plan to stay there for a long time. It is extremely important to be familiar with the real estate market in your area. This is especially important for house flippers whose goal is a quick sale after a rehab project rather than waiting for the home to appreciate over time.

> **Builder Alert: Know your local real estate market. The home's value after construction is extremely important. You do not want to put more money into a home than you can get out of it.**

Home Equity Loans

A home equity loan is the easiest way to finance a major renovation project. Unlike many construction loans, there are no escrow fees for this type of loan, only the fees associated with obtaining the loan. With a home equity loan, you are in complete control of the money. An appraisal is required for a home equity loan, but these are usually more streamlined "drive-by" appraisals, not the kind you would need for a regular mortgage.

There are three basic types of home equity loans: fixed-rate, home equity lines of credit, and cash-out refinance loans, though cash-out refinancing is best used only in certain circumstances when you can consolidate your loans with a lower interest rate or want to pay off some other bills. Fixed-rate home equity loans have a fixed interest rate and are for a predetermined amount of money that is given to the borrower in a lump sum. Home equity lines of credit (HELOCs) approve the borrower to take out money up to a certain amount whenever needed. The borrower will receive checks that allow them to draw on the loan; each check they write lowers the balance available. HELOCs work like credit cards, but at much lower rates. These are nice because the borrower only pays interest on what they have drawn, not on the entire amount, which might sit in a bank account for months before it is used. HELOCs also have the added benefit of being paid down as you make payments, making more money available to you as you pay them off, just as with a credit card. HELOCs are also nice because you can just write a check to someone when you need to or even write a check to yourself and deposit the money into your bank account. Paying your contractors, even large sums of money, is just as easy as writing a check.

However, HELOCs usually have variable interest rates. If interest rates increase dramatically over time, you could wind up paying a lot more on a monthly basis than you originally thought. HELOCs are also usually interest-only loans, meaning you are only required to pay the interest on the balance of your loan each month. While this is nice in the short term, because it gives you a lower payment than a traditional principal-and-interest loan during the construction phase, you do not want to fall into the habit of only making the minimum interest payments. Most home equity loans are for twenty years. If you borrow $100,000 and only make the interest payments for twenty years, you will have not paid off the original balance and will still owe $100,000. If that loan does not get paid off, the bank can take your house unless you refinance the loan. The best way to avoid this is to calculate what the loan payment would be with both principal and interest and submit that as your HELOC payment every month, or you can get a new mortgage after construction is complete, combining your first mortgage and the home equity loan. Interest rates will determine when it is best to do this; however, your new mortgage will require an appraisal, so your home will need to have increased in value enough to wrap the home equity loan into the new mortgage. This is why it is important to know your local real estate market and make sure your renovation project does not price you out of the ability to refinance, especially in the case of an expensive addition.

Home equity loans are usually given up to 80 percent of the equity in a home, although some banks will lend up to 90 percent. If you have a $200,000 home but still owe $100,000, then you have $100,000 in equity. That means you can only get a home equity loan for $80,000 to $90,000. That is usually plenty for most renovation projects but might not cover the cost of a major addition. That is when you need a construction loan.

Construction Loans

Construction loans are used for financing large new construction projects. Construction loans are based on the amount needed to build the house, and the home is appraised based on its future value after the project is completed. Construction loans are only for short periods of time and typically have higher interest rates. Homeowners have to refinance out of them into a conventional mortgage once the project is complete. Banks issue construction loans more than other types of mortgage companies, because construction loans are kept in house until the project is complete and a new mortgage obtained, not sold to the secondary mortgage market right away as with most conventional loans. For this reason, start with banks when researching construction loans.

There are two types of construction loans. A one-time close loan combines the initial line of credit needed to fund the project with the final conventional mortgage when the project is completed. These are sometimes known as convertible loans. The fewer closings associated with these loans mean fewer fees than with multiple loans; however, these loans are usually for a predetermined amount. If your project winds up costing more than expected, the loan amount cannot be increased; a new loan will be needed. Lenders are sometimes unwilling to give these loans to owners acting as their own general contractors because they are worried the owners might not be able to estimate all the expenses accurately (Heldmann 2006, 42). Check with lenders to find out their requirements and if they allow the borrower to act as their own general contractor.

There are also two-close construction loans, in which the loan needed for construction is separate from the end loan, which is a regular mortgage. These loans require two separate closings and therefore have separate sets of costs associated with closing the two loans, but they are more flexible and allow the borrower to easily increase the amount needed during the construction phase as long as the borrower meets the income requirements to qualify for the higher-than-expected loan amount.

Construction loans can include the purchase of the lot when building on vacant land. They also work somewhat like a home equity line of credit where the money is distributed as needed rather than given to the borrower all at once. You are also usually only required to pay the interest on construction loans as the project progresses, as with a HELOC. With construction loans, money is disbursed in phases, known as payouts or draws. One payout might cover the excavation and foundation, another the framing and roofing, another roughing in the mechanicals, et cetera, until the project is complete. If you get a construction loan, make sure you understand the payout schedule and how the payouts correspond to the money you will have to pay your contractors and pay for materials and other products that go into a home. It is always good to have plenty of cash on hand to pay for things between loan dispersals, when expenses can pile up.

Money from the construction loan is usually deposited into an escrow account, and contractors are paid from that account. One downside to a construction loan is that if an extra payout is needed, the lender or escrow company might charge a hefty fee. Make sure you ask about this if you get a construction loan.

Lenders use their own inspectors to evaluate the progress of the project and will not distribute money for the next phase of construction until the prior phase is completed properly. These are not municipal building inspectors but inspectors the bank uses for the purpose of the loan. Find out how soon after an inspection you can receive your next draw from the bank.

Regardless of the type of construction loan, the lender will require a lot of construction documentation to process the loan, aside from the financial documents of the borrower. General contractors are used to supplying all the necessary cost estimates, completion schedules, and other paperwork to the bank, but if the borrower/homeowner is acting as the general contractor, they need to be familiar with all the documentation the bank will require. This is not an impossible task; it just takes time to get all the documents together in a format the bank will accept. Again, it is best to have a long sit-down with your lender and go over in detail everything that will be required for the loan. Have all forms and documentation nicely typed and formatted. Some items needed for the loan include:

- an estimate of the project total (including bids from subcontractors);
- cost of the building permits;
- a survey of the property;
- the architect's blueprints;
- cost estimate of materials not included in subcontractors' bids;
- the names and contact information of all subcontractors and building supply houses;
- a schedule or timeline of the project;
- proof of added liability insurance; and
- a personal statement or professional resume that stresses construction or project management experience.

The construction loan covers the costs of building the home, but things like the survey, added liability insurance, the architect's fee, building permits, et cetera are expenses that might have to be covered before you receive any money from the loan. For this reason, you must have a decent amount of start-up money on hand before even going to the bank. A detailed cost-estimate sheet will not only help you set and manage your budget but also give you an idea of how much start-up money you need and provide you with a detailed estimate for your lender. Bankrate has a good website explaining construction loans (Marquit 2020).

If you cannot qualify for a construction loan until you sell your current home, you might consider a bridge loan so you can start construction while you wait for your current home to sell. A bridge loan is a short-term loan taken out against your current property to finance the purchase of a new home. Bridge loans are usually for six to twelve months and access your current home's equity. These loans are used in competitive housing markets when buyers want to make an offer without any contingencies. However, they are risky. If your current home does sell during the contractual period, you might be stuck with two mortgage payments or have to pay the bridge loan off in full. Bridge loans also carry high interest rates, and you need enough equity in your current home to qualify. If you do not want to take out a bridge loan, you will have to wait until your home sells and find a temporary place to live until your new home is ready.

Financing Kitchens

Most people include the cost of a new kitchen in their construction or home equity loan when building a new home or addition. Home equity loans can also be taken out for smaller remodeling projects that might include a new kitchen in an existing home. Many kitchen remodeling stores and large home improvement centers offer financing options just for kitchens that are separate from their store credit cards. Big-box stores such as Lowe's offer installment plans over a fixed number of years, typically three, five, or seven. The loans also carry much lower interest rates than their typical store credit cards. Normal purchases on their credit cards might have the same interest rates as regular credit cards, or higher, but their kitchen financing plans carry a much lower rate, close to 7 percent or 8 percent at the time of this writing. You would never want to put a $25,000 kitchen on a high-rate credit card, but the rates for these kitchen installment loans are much lower and might be closer to the rates on a home equity loan.

These installment loans are also much easier to take out than a home equity loan. In fact, qualifying for these loans is usually part of the store credit card you might already have. It is usually just a matter of being billed differently for the kitchen project than a regular store purchase. These loans can also cover the cost of the kitchen installation when using the store's installers. A $25,000 kitchen loan would be like taking out a car loan.

Even though the interest rates are higher than those of the end-loan mortgage after building a house or an addition, do not rule out installment loans for kitchens if you can afford a few hundred dollars extra per month. The reason has to do with interest and the total amount paid over time. If you pay back a kitchen loan over a few years, as with a car payment, you will pay far less in interest than you would if you borrowed the $25,000 on a regular mortgage or home equity loan and paid it off over twenty or thirty years with the rest of your house. You would never buy a car with a home equity loan and take twenty years to pay it off, even though the payments would be far lower. You will also have $25,000 more in equity in your home if you finance the kitchen separately.

At the time of writing, Lowe's had a fixed-rate installment plan for purchases over $2,000 as part of their Advantage Card store credit program. They even have an online payment calculator to help you figure out your monthly payment. Other stores offer similar payment options. Using their current APR and their online payment calculator, consider this example comparing a kitchen financed through Lowe's at a higher rate to adding it to a thirty-year mortgage end loan.

Loan Type	Loan Amount	Interest / APR	Number of Payments	Monthly Payment	Total Cost
Mortgage	$25,000	4.0%	360	$119.35	$42,966
Store Loan	$25,000	7.99%	84	$390	$32,760

As you can see, putting the kitchen on your mortgage would save you $270.65 per month, but the total cost of the kitchen over thirty years would be $42,966. Compare this to $32,760 for the fixed-rate store loan for seven years. Over the life of the mortgage, you would wind up paying $17,966 in interest over the original cost of the kitchen and $10,206 more than had you financed it for seven years, even at the higher rate.

Chapter 6
Executing Your Plan

*Some failure in life is inevitable. It is impossible to live
without failing at something, unless you live so cautiously
that you might as well not have lived at all—in which case,
you fail by default.*

—J. K. Rowling

Now that you have your permits, estimates, financing, and contractors
lined up and are ready to begin your project, you need to determine the
order in which the phases of your project will be completed and make
sure no important details have been left out. Consult the planning and
preconstruction checklists on the following pages before you get started.
Keep in mind the springtime brings rain that can delay a project if
excavation and foundation work is needed. Likewise, if work is to begin
as winter approaches, plan to start early enough so any excavation work
can take place before the ground freezes and the foundation is poured
before the onset of freezing temperatures. You will also have to arrange
for temporary heaters during the winter months until the heating system
is up and running. You might also need a temporary generator to supply
power if electricity is not yet available. Make sure the major
landscaping—trees, bushes, and shrubs—is done next to last and your
driveway, sidewalks, and custom garage doors are done last. With your
property being a construction site for months, you do not want your new
driveway or custom garage doors damaged or stained by construction
equipment, dirt, or cars and trucks that might leak oil. Roll-off dumpsters
have also been known to crack driveways, so play it safe and complete
these items last. Sod for new grass should be the only thing left to put in
after your driveway and sidewalks are poured.

In new construction, underground utilities will have to be piped to
the site and laid before the foundation is poured. These usually come
into the house through the foundation slab if there is no basement.
Otherwise, they are brought through the foundation walls, either through
a sleeve placed in the walls as the foundation is poured or drilled through

the foundation walls and sealed with hydraulic cement before the foundation is waterproofed. Waterproofing should be done by a company that specializes in waterproofing foundations and will warranty their work. This can be very important when building an addition in which the new foundation meets the old foundation. The waterproofing company should fill the joints with an epoxy compound.

It can take twenty-eight days for concrete to fully harden, or cure. This is the safest time to start the next phase of building, though some builders start backfilling and building when the foundation is 50 percent cured. This usually takes about seven days (Allen n.d.). Colder temperatures can result in longer curing times. Check your local building codes and inspection requirements. The hydration process needed for curing virtually stops at temperatures at or below 40 degrees Fahrenheit (Palmer 2020). Driveways need about seven days before you can drive on them, though some contractors say to wait several days longer if you have a large vehicle or pickup truck (Taylor n.d. (b); Taylor and Vila n.d.).

Make sure you have coordinated a timeline with your subcontractors so they know when you will need them, and make sure you have ordered and arranged for the delivery of materials in advance so they can be delivered when needed. Contractors do not like having to wait around; lost time is lost money for them. If your project is delayed too much, your subcontractors could take other jobs, and you will have to wait until they have time for you again, which pushes the timetable back for everyone else. Everyone has to do their part according to the timeline laid out.

Older homes were made out of structural brick with solid brick walls that supported the structure. Some new brick homes, some additions, and many commercial structures are built using concrete blocks, which are then covered with face brick. In these cases, the masonry work is completed after the foundation is poured. Most brick homes today are built using face brick over wood framing. In this case, rough framing comes after the foundation work.

Preconstruction Checklist

1. Check your local building codes to see if it is permissible for a homeowner to act as their own general contractor.
2. Talk to various banks and lending institutions to see if they allow the homeowner (the borrower) to act as the general contractor and if they finance land.
3. Obtain a survey of the property.
4. Locate and mark utility lines.
5. Have your sewer lines and catch basin (if you have one) scoped by a plumber with a camera to determine where your lines run and where the best place would be to connect the new sewer lines for your addition ($300-$400).
6. If there is a catch basin that needs to be moved or can be eliminated, make sure no other drains or downspouts flow into it that might need to be rerouted.
7. Hire an architect.
8. Decide if you want to use a general contractor.
9. Talk to your insurance company about obtaining extra liability insurance.
10. Obtain lien wavier and sworn statement forms.
11. Decide if you are going to move or live through the construction.
12. Apply for permits.
13. Line up a cleaning crew and crew to help with moving items.
14. Rent dumpsters for your project (thirty-cubic-yard size).
15. Find a company that provides construction fencing.
16. Find a company to provide a portable toilet for workers.
17. Determine if you will need a new hot water tank to meet the demands of a new bathroom or jacuzzi tub.
18. Plan for temporary heat and electricity if needed.
19. Set start date with first construction crew and make sure dumpster, fencing, and porta potty will be on site for them.
20. Make sure structural steel is delivered and can be unloaded and put into place with the necessary equipment.
21. Type and go over any special notes or instructions with subcontractors, such as placement of drains or outlets for jacuzzi tubs, towel warmers, or anything else that might not be detailed on the blueprints.

Order of Operations Guide

1. Locate and mark utilities.
2. If building an addition, board up any windows you want protected.
3. Demolition.
4. Excavation.
5. Sewer work, including any septic systems and sump and ejector pump pits.
6. Underground utilities, such as gas and water piped to site.
7. Foundation and drain tile.
8. Waterproofing of foundation.
9. Rough framing and roof sheathing.
10. House wrap, such as Tyvek.
11. Masonry, chimneys, stucco, siding, et cetera.
12. Roofing: flashing, waterproof membranes, facia, soffits, gutters, shingles, tile, slate, et cetera.
13. Windows and exterior doors (consider using cheap, temporary doors to close off entrances until work is done).
14. HVAC and venting systems for kitchens and baths.
15. Rough plumbing, gas lines, and hot water tank.
16. Rough electrical.
17. Insulation.
18. Drywall/plaster and cement board under tile in wet areas.
19. Flooring and tile.
20. Kitchen and bath cabinets and fixtures.
21. Finish plumbing of sinks, toilets, showers, and bathtubs.
22. Trim carpentry: interior doors, millwork, moldings, casings, et cetera.
23. Kitchen countertops (measured after cabinets installed).
24. Backsplash tile.
25. Paint.
26. Finish electrical (trim): outlets, switches, and lighting.
27. Landscaping: bushes, shrubs, and trees.
28. Driveway and sidewalks (install sod after these items).
29. Appliances.
30. Carpeting.
31. Window treatments.
32. Enjoy your home.

Chapter 7
Basements

The people who are crazy enough to think they can change the world are the ones who do.

—Steve Jobs

Basements, new or old, can be fantastic places to add more space to your home. Gone are the days of old, dark, musty basements with cheap paneling. Today's basements are being transformed into beautiful living spaces that rival the finished look of any beautiful first floor. Depending on how the basement is laid out, the large open spaces of basements make great areas for playrooms, home theaters, game rooms, wine cellars, home gyms, workshops, hobby rooms, indoor pools and spas, home offices, et cetera. In fact, the internet and magazines are full of great ideas to create amazing spaces for the entire family. When it comes to basements, the sky is the limit, given the right amount of space and money.

Basements are common in older homes, especially in colder climates, because foundations usually have to be dug several feet below ground past the frost line, even for a crawl space. If that much earth has already been removed, it does not cost much more to dig down a little farther to excavate a full basement with a proper ceiling height. Basements also serve as a place to locate mechanical equipment away from the living space and run piping throughout the house. This was especially true in bygone days, when it was common for homes to have oil or coal-fired furnaces. In fact, many old homes had a coal room in the basement where coal was shoveled in through a window. Other old homes had a pipe that ran from the basement boiler room underground to the property near the street, where an oil truck would deliver oil by connecting to the pipe and pumping the oil into a tank. Basements were never meant to be pretty or used as living space, but, if done right, even old basements can greatly increase a home's living area.

For a while, in the 1990s especially, it seemed newer homes were not being built with basements. Many new homes were simply built on a crawl space or slab, and if a homeowner wanted a basement, it was a big upgrade. Many people who bought homes without basements regretted it later as they were left with no place to store things and no option to increase living space down the road like people who had basements. In some parts of the country, where the water table is high and the ground is soft and wet or hard and rocky, as in the Southwest, basements are still not common because of the added costs of excavation and extra structural requirements. But basements can still be built in most locations, depending on one's budget. In the long run, a basement is usually well worth the investment. It is also worth considering using metal wall studs to frame the basement. They are resistant to water, and it is easy to pull electrical, internet, and audio/visual cables through the premade slots in the studs.

Basement Water Problems

Two of the biggest problems with basements are low ceilings and moisture. A damp, musty basement is noticeable immediately to the trained eye and nose and a sure red flag to prospective home buyers and those who want to transform their basements into nice living spaces. Fortunately, waterproofing has come a long way. Under normal circumstances, proper waterproofing of the foundation and proper drainage around the house can prevent moisture and water infiltration. Drain tile is typically installed around the perimeter of the foundation near the footings to collect groundwater when it rains. The drain tile, usually perforated PVC, corrugated pipe, or clay tile, directs water away from the foundation to prevent the buildup of hydrostatic water pressure, which leads to cracks in the foundation and seepage. The drain tile directs water into a sump pit in the basement, where a sump pump pumps the water into the sewer line where it flows into the municipal sewer system or the outside of the house. (Check your local building codes. Chicago uses a combined waste and storm sewer system. Other localities have separate sewer systems for waste and storm water.)

As an additional measure of safety, install interior drain tiles around the inside perimeter of the foundation by the footings. This is often done in existing homes as a way to fix seepage problems from hydrostatic pressure when it would be too costly and destructive to excavate around the outside of a house to repair exterior drain tile. This is important if that would involve digging up patios, sidewalks, driveways, et cetera. Interior drain tile has an added benefit: it can be coupled with plastic drainage boards on the inside walls of the foundation to direct any water that might penetrate down into the drain tile and prevent it from spilling out onto the floor or under a finished wall. (We had to do this to solve some of the water problems in our basement.)

There are companies that specialize in waterproofing foundation walls by applying a moisture barrier to the inside or outside walls. On new construction, this is easily done on the outside when the foundation is still accessible before the soil has been backfilled. Flood control systems that block sewer water from backing up into the house during heavy rains are also common. In short, if everything is done properly, a new basement should not have any water problems. Still, there are several ways water can cause problems in a new or old basement:

- seepage caused by hydrostatic pressure;
- seepage caused by cracks in the foundation;
- cracked drain tiles or gutter downspout tiles;
- flooding when sewers back up during storms;
- no drains or faulty drains in window wells;
- faulty tuckpointing;
- basement windows not sealed properly;
- gaps around water pipes or electrical conduit running to the outside that allow water to drip in when it rains;
- faulty sump pumps;
- improper drainage around the house because of problems with gutters; and
- improper drainage around the house because the soil is too high where the foundation meets the brick or siding exterior, causing water to spill over the foundation.

Unfortunately, in our situation, we were getting water in our basement in every way possible. In fact, when I was growing up in the home, water had come into the basement every time it rained for years. Each of these situations had to be addressed. If they were not, not only would we never be able to finish our basement into extra living space, but the damage from the water, which was plainly visible, would continue to get worse and cause serious structural, mold, and water corrosion issues. We did not know how bad the situation was until we got in there and ripped out the old knotty pine walls. Every time we thought we had solved the problem, we noticed water coming in from somewhere else when it rained. Remarkably, the biggest fix required installing drain tile around the inside perimeter of the foundation and running drains from the window wells through the foundation and down to the new drain from the inside. This stopped the biggest cause of water infiltration because the old window wells were built without drains. During heavy rains, they would fill up like bathtubs, and water would pour in through the windows. Installing interior drain tile was an enormously destructive project that required jackhammering the basement floor to install the drain tile and direct the water into the sump pit, then pouring new gravel and cement in the basement. Fortunately, this was all done in one day, along with fixing one crack in the foundation. (Most cracks can now be fixed from the inside.)

I should also note that we received an estimate of over $9,000 from a reputable national waterproofing company to install the interior drain tile. They also told us we needed a new sump pit. We got the job done for less than $3,000 by a local franchised waterproofing company that charged about $100 per liner foot to install the drain tile. They also only charged $100 to replace the old sump pump with a new pump with a battery backup, which I purchased separately. We never needed a new pit. This is another reason it pays to shop around and get several estimates.

We also had to install new glass block windows in the window wells, relandscape around the house to lower the level of the dirt around the foundation, tuckpoint the bricks on the inside and outside of the basement, remove the old hose spigot and electrical conduit pipe running outside, and fill the gaps in the bricks. Since this was done, we have never gotten a single drop of water in the basement. With the exception of the interior drain tile that had to be installed, all the other fixes were relatively easy once the interior walls were down. The old knotty pine walls, a staple of 1960s and 1970s basement finishing, had to go anyway. The new drywall combined with the original plaster walls, new floating floor, and wood molding created a bright, finished look. The can lighting we installed brightened up the entire basement without taking up ceiling height, though it was a messy job cutting into the ceiling to retrofit the new can lights.

Basement Ceiling Height

Another problem with basements is low ceilings. Unsightly plumbing and bad lighting in old basements can all be replaced or relocated, albeit at a price, but low ceilings can be a major problem for any basement. Unfortunately, many very old homes have really low ceilings, and many builders are more concerned with building new homes as cheaply and quickly as possible. With proper planning, the problem of low basement ceilings can be avoided in new basements, and, though it's very costly, many people are now fixing this problem in older homes by removing the basement floor, digging deeper, and repouring a new, lower floor.

When building a new home with a basement, it is important to excavate deep enough to have high ceilings. The extra money to excavate for eight- to nine-foot ceilings will be well worth it. Some people might think that is too much, but keep in mind that your home is probably going to have ductwork for an HVAC system, steel beams, and water piping. These mechanical features can hang a foot or so from the ceiling if they run under a beam, taking up valuable height. Drop ceilings are often installed to conceal the machinal equipment, but these hang down even lower and eat up more space. Therefore, it is best to plan for a high ceiling, especially if you plan to have exercise equipment or other items that might require a full-height ceiling. When we built our addition, we dug out the new basement area about a foot deeper than the existing basement to allow for a higher ceiling. It is a step down to the new basement, but it gave us the headroom we needed for our exercise equipment. We also had to install a second sump pump just for the new basement. Since it was at a lower level, we could not run the drain tile "uphill" to the existing sump pump.

In older basements, there is a way to fix the ceiling height problem that is becoming more common with people who find a house they love and want a modern basement. Many homeowners are actually digging out their basement floor and lowering it to provide more headroom. There are companies that specialize in doing just this, and the internet and YouTube are full of videos showing this process. It involves jackhammering up the concrete basement floor, digging down to the desired depth, and pouring a new concrete floor. Of course, it is not this simple. The foundation has to be underpinned with new footings and new foundation walls, and water and sewer pipes might have to be moved. If the basement has posts supporting a steel beam, new posts have to be installed that extend down to the new floor, and the house will have to be supported by hydraulic jacks while the work is being done. This is a labor-intensive project because so much of the excavating and removal of debris has to be done by hand or with small excavators and conveyor belts. However, the results can be amazing, though this is only recommended for people who plan to stay in their homes for a very long time as they probably will not recoup the cost. But if you find a big, beautiful old home you love, it just might be worth the cost and effort.

In any basement, drywalling the ceiling instead of installing a drop ceiling adds a clean, finished look that is more homey and less commercial looking. A high ceiling will make it easier to install drywall under any mechanicals and still have enough headroom. Pipes that might protrude will blend in if painted the color of the ceiling.

Other Design Considerations

The forced-air central heating and cooling systems in new homes are typically placed in the center of the basement to increase efficiency so that duct runs emanate out from a center point since long runs and bends in the ductwork decrease airflow to the more distant parts of the house. While this makes sense from an HVAC point of view, locating the furnace in the middle of the basement creates some design challenges and can interrupt the wide-open benefits of a finished basement. Add to this the fact that most basements in a typical new 2,500-square-foot home are not that big to begin with when you consider there is almost never a basement under the attached garage.

If you want open space in the basement and do not want to design around the furnace, you can request that it be located off to the side if your HVAC contractor does not think it will greatly impair its functionality, given the layout of your home. If you have a large home, you can install two separate HVAC systems so that one system does not have to service the entire house, thereby making the system more efficient and eliminating long duct runs. (A second system is often put in the attic to service the second floor only.)

Another solution to avoid locating the furnace in the middle of the basement is not to install a forced-air system. In older homes, the boilers were often located off to the side of the basement. Since hot water was circulating through pipes, strong airflow to vents on the far side of the house was not an issue. If you install a hot-water heating system in your new house or addition, such as radiant floor heat, you can purchase a boiler that literally hangs on an outside wall and pumps water to the entire house. If you combine this with a small-duct high-velocity air-conditioning system located in the attic, you will not lose precious real estate in the basement. You will also have the best heating and air-conditioning system available. There is more about this in Chapter 12, but this is exactly what we did in our addition. We added a new basement under the new kitchen. The new basement room was not huge, but it was enough for a small workout area and a workshop/hobby room. If we had installed central air and heat in the addition, we would have had to locate the system in the new basement, which would have destroyed the new space we wanted. We also located the sump pump for the new basement under a new utility staircase that comes down from the new garage, so it, too, is out of the way.

Another great way to dramatically increase the size of a new basement is to add basement space under an attached garage if your local building codes allow this. This is very rarely done because it is not allowed by code in some areas and, if it is allowed, requires a lot of extra structural work to support the cars above. The space will require steel-reinforced foundation walls; pre-engineered concrete floors with flexicore for the garage floor (flexicore is steel-reinforced concrete used in the construction of multistory buildings); a crane to lift the flexicore slabs into place; and proper sealing of the garage floor to prevent water, gasoline, and other liquids from seeping to the basement below. This might seem daunting; however, if done, you can easily add over four hundred square feet of space to a basement under a typical two-car garage.

Another consideration for a new basement is access to an outside staircase. When people think of walk-out basements today, they often think of glass doors than open out onto a beautiful sloping lot. Most homes do not have sloping lots to make this possible, but outside access to the basement is a convenience well worth planning for in advance. I have been in homes in which the basement door is in a tight hallway opposite a wall with no way to navigate large items down the stairs. Outside basement stairways are common in older homes. They are not as common in new homes unless requested, but they make life so much easier when you are trying to get mechanical equipment, appliances, and other large items into the basement. They also make it much easier to bring building materials in to finish the basement. Older homes typically just had concrete stairs that went down a few steps to a basement door. Some homes had the steps covered with old-fashioned storm cellar doors, which are great for extra security and to keep rain and snow out.

When we built our addition on the back of the house, we lost our back door, which had a landing that went up to the first floor and down the basement. It was hard enough to get large objects around the corner and down to the basement. Losing the ability to come in from the outside would doom our ability to get large objects downstairs, so I knew I wanted another staircase to the basement. Rather than excavate around the house somewhere to build a new outside entrance, I told the architect I wanted to incorporate a new staircase from the new garage down to the new basement. This was not negotiable. The challenge was finding a place to put it where it would not be in the way. Some creative engineering solved the problem. However, when installing outside stairs to the basement, there must be a drain connected to the sewer system at the base of the stairs, even if the stairs are covered with storm cellar doors. The only way around this is completely enclosing the stairs as part of the house.

Builder Alert: Be sure to include a drain at the base of any outside staircase to the basement.

If you are spending the money to build a new basement, make sure it has a bathroom. This will add a tremendous amount of convenience and resale value to the home, even if you never finish the basement yourself. If you do not want to spend the money to finish the basement and bathroom right away, make sure you have the plumbing for the bathroom roughed in when the home is built where you think it would make sense to place a basement bathroom. That way, when you are ready, all you have to do is put up the walls around the bathroom and connect the fixtures to the pipes. Roughing in a basement bathroom includes running hot and cold water lines for the sink and toilet (and shower if you want one) and sewer drain pipes for the fixtures. In many old homes, basement bathrooms were just connected to the sewer lines running under the basement floor, and/or toilets were often raised up a step or two to provide the necessary downward pitch for the waste to flow into the sewer pipes. The elevated toilet was also to help prevent flooding if the sewers backed up during a rainstorm. In most municipalities today, basement bathroom drains in new and old homes must be connected to an ejector pit and pump. These pits are like sump pump pits, but they are sealed to keep odors and sewer gas contained. The ejector pump grinds up liquid and solid waste material and pumps it up and out to the sewer line to prevent flooding if the sewers back up during a heavy rain. The ejector pit should be roughed in with all the other plumbing at the time of construction to eliminate the need to hack up the basement floor at a later date.

The great thing about basements is they are naturally climate controlled. Because they are built below ground, they are naturally warmer in the winter and cooler in the summer. In fact, and though I know people might disagree, I would never insulate a basement again. When we finished the basement in our previous home, a Chicago bungalow, I installed insulation before the drywall. Before we finished the basement, it was always cool down there in the summer and comfortable enough in the winter. However, after we finished it, it was always freezing in the winter and very warm and humid in the summer. Sealing the basement with the insulation interfered with the natural cooling and warming effect of the ground outside the basement walls. When we moved into our current home, the basement was partially finished: half with drywall when the basement was partially remodeled after an electrical fire in the 1990s and half with the old knotty pine. There was no insulation at all in the basement, and when we refinished it, I kept it like that. The basement breathes and still stays cool in the summer and warm in the winter.

That being said, it does not take much to heat or cool a basement. If you are having a home built with central air and heat, make sure that vents are included for the basement and that the basement ductwork is on a separate climate zone from the rest of the house. Basements with large open areas can also be cooled with mini-split air-conditioning systems or with small-duct high-velocity systems that serve the rest of the house. Basements are easily heated with baseboard heat, European-style panel radiators, or hydronic radiant floor heat installed before the concrete slab floor is poured or in a new subfloor above the slab. Covering the entire basement with radiant floor heat can be expensive and possibly overkill for most basements, but there is no better heat.

Lastly, every basement should be equipped with a radon detector, which you can buy at most hardware stores or home centers. Radon is a naturally occurring radioactive gas that emanates from the soil or groundwater, making basements particularly susceptible. Radon can cause lung cancer; it is odorless, colorless, and tasteless and can only be detected by testing for it. If your home has high levels of radon, you will need to call a licensed radon reduction contractor. These specialists are certified through the EPA or state agencies.

Remember, when it comes to finishing basements, the sky is the limit, so talk to your architect and scour the internet for ideas for your dream basement that will meet your family's current and future needs.

Basement Renovation Photographs

Figure 9 The front of the basement had the most water damage. Notice the streaks on the floor where water would enter from behind the knotty pine paneling, then follow the slope in the floor toward the drain in the boiler room. A window well on the far side of the stone fireplace was the biggest source of water infiltration, but water was also spilling over the foundation behind the paneling. The awful commercial-style tile floor was installed in the 1990s after a fire in the basement and was impossible to keep clean. The original ceiling radiators supply ample heat. One is on each side of the existing basement.

Figure 10. These photos reveal the improper drainage around the house caused by the height of the soil over the foundation. The soil was covering the bricks and causing water to seep through the mortar into the basement when it rained. Decades of new dirt for landscaping and roots from evergreen bushes and trees raised the soil levels around the house. The soil was regraded and the bricks tuckpointed.

Figure 11. Once the knotty pine was removed, the extent of the water damage was revealed. Water would collect in the window well, which had no drain, then pour in through the window vent. It also deteriorated the seal around the window and came through the sides. The standing water on the floor caused the efflorescence on the stone fireplace and left mold on the knotty pine. In the right corner was an electrical conduit that was completely rusted away, revealing old cloth wiring that was completely bare . . . a major fire hazard.

Figure 12. After the knotty pine was removed, it was easy to spot where the water was leaking in through the bricks above the concrete foundation when it rained because the soil was too high around the house. The other corner also had an electrical conduit that had rusted away from the water damage.

Figure 13. Knotty pine was removed from these walls, revealing a pretty Spanish stucco plaster design. The moisture damage extended around to the left side of the fireplace and rotted the bottom of these plaster walls. Notice the water damage to the wall under the window in the boiler room in the background where another window well with no drain was located.

Figure 14. The perimeter of the basement had to be hacked up to install interior drain tile that would direct groundwater toward the sump pump. Gravel was installed over the PVC drain tile before new cement was poured over the trench.

Figure 15. A drainpipe connected to a drain in the window well was brought through the basement wall in the boiler room and down into new interior drain tile where it flowed into the sump pump. The same thing was done for the other window well by the fireplace.

Figure 16. Notice the PVC drain tile under the gravel. Drains were installed in the window wells outside the house, then PVC piping was brought through the wall below the window where it ran down the wall and connected to the drain tile in the floor. The window well water could then drain into the sump pit. The new finished wall was built out to conceal the PVC piping.

Figure 17. This is the remodeled front of the basement where all the knotty pine was located. Built-in wall speakers complete the home theater. A floating wood-grain laminate floor was installed over the concrete floor, making for a soft feel. Wall sconces and new can lights were added. With technology constantly changing so rapidly, make sure your electrician runs all audio/visual and ethernet wires in conduit so new wires can be pulled in the future.

Figure 18. The wood-burning stone fireplace was cleaned and the efflorescence removed. Efflorescence is a residual salt buildup that accumulates on brick, stone, cement, mortar, and other porous materials after excess moisture evaporates. Efflorescence can be removed by scrubbing the brick with a stiff brush, rinsing it with water or distilled white vinegar, power washing, or using a chemical cleaner, depending on the severity of the buildup.

Figure 19. The interior plaster wall that was previously covered with knotty pine was repaired, leaving a pretty stucco design in the basement that matches the design in the upstairs living room.

Figure 20. The laundry room was originally the kitchen. It also had a step-up bathroom and a pantry closet. The bathroom was not very nice or practical, and with the glass block window located there, it was the best place to cut through to the new basement. Upon demoing the pantry, we discovered there had originally been a shower there. The plan was to relocate the bathroom to where the pantry was and use the old bathroom as a hallway to the new basement.

Figure 21. The awkward original bathroom off the laundry room was moved to the right where the pantry was to make room for a hallway to the new basement, which can be seen beyond the door. The pantry door was replaced by a wall behind where the basement refrigerator is now located, and the bathroom door is in the new hallway.

Figure 22. View of the old bathroom window from the new basement before the cut-through. The window was above ground before this area was excavated for the new basement.

Figure 23. Underground piping can be seen for the relocated basement bathroom.

Figure 24. Newly poured cement for relocated basement bathroom.

Figure 25. New basement bathroom.

Chapter 8
Garages

*A person should set his goals as early as he can and devote
all his energy and talent to getting there. With enough
effort, he may achieve it. Or he may find something that is
even more rewarding. But in the end, no matter what the
outcome, he will know he has been alive.*

—Walt Disney

Garages are not just for cars and lawn mowers anymore. Like basements, garages have come a long way in the last couple of decades. With proper planning, garages can be decked out into plush spaces. As with basements, the sky is the limit, given enough space and money. Even modest garages can be transformed into usable space that is functional and comfortable. Attached garages with the garage doors facing the side look like part of the house rather than a garage. (Side-facing garages typically require about twenty feet of space on the side of the house for the driveway.) Stylish carriage-house garage doors and attractive driveway pavers can make a garage look like a beautiful part of any home.

A whole host of storage cabinets, shelving, flooring, and workbenches can make garages the perfect place to store tools, bikes, and other items. Garage heaters add warmth while making it possible to comfortably use the garage year-round. If you have enough ceiling height, storage lift systems make it possible to store bicycles, boxes, and other items out of the way; car lifts make it possible to increase the number of cars that fit into a garage. Car lifts require a high ceiling if you want to park two SUVs on top of one another, but less headroom is needed for sedans. Installing car lifts also requires high-lift rails and a wall-mounted garage door opener. Car lifts can also be used to store yard equipment and other large items, such as snow blowers, tractors, ATVs, et cetera. People just have more stuff now compared to many years ago. If possible, a three-car garage is well worth the extra money to make the storing of lawn equipment, patio furniture, bikes, toys, and other items much easier. If you plan on installing any type of car lift, make sure the poured concrete floor meets the minimum requirements specified by the manufacturer.

Underground Garages

Underground garages are growing in popularity, especially in urban areas where land is at a premium and lots are small. They are also a great way to increase living and yard space by not having a garage take up a huge chunk of the house or yard. The easiest basement garages to build are those tucked under a home situated on a sloping lot. Otherwise, a full-blown underground garage will be needed. These are not terribly complicated to build—not much different from a basement—but they require proper planning, and they can cause as many issues as they solve. If basements in your area are not common because of the composition of the soil, a basement garage might not be feasible or could require a lot of engineering. Otherwise, a basement garage can be incorporated into the design of a new home or addition along with the rest of the basement. Of course, basement garages are a lot more expensive to build than traditional aboveground garages because of all the excavation and foundation work.

The two biggest challenges for basement garages are the space needed for the driveway and sufficient drains to collect rainwater and channel it into the sewer system so that the garage does not flood. Indoor garage drains are not allowed in many municipalities anymore for fear of leaking oil or gasoline entering the drain. Therefore, you will need to install a channel drain, also called a trench drain, along the outside of the garage door. It will have to be big enough to handle all the rain running down the driveway during a heavy storm. Depending on the location of your sewer lines, this could require a lot of excavation. In colder climates, snow and ice are also major concerns, so the driveway will also have to be heated using a radiant heating system that circulates hot water under the driveway. The hot water PEX tubing is laid before the concrete is poured and melts the ice. If you do not already have a radiant heating system or plan on having one in your home, this is an expensive necessity. If you already have a radiant floor heating system or are building one with your new home or addition, then it is simply a matter of creating a separate heating zone for the driveway.

When designing your underground garage, you have to excavate deep enough for tall SUVs. You will probably need at least eight or nine feet of clear headroom; however, the more ceiling height you require, the deeper you have to excavate. This will require a longer driveway that slopes down gently rather than a steep hill heading down into the garage. The need for a longer driveway is a common problem. Keep in mind, if your home is built a few feet above ground level, this lessens the depth you have to excavate because there will already be some built-in headroom under the first level of the home. For example, if you have steps going up to your house, and the first floor is three feet above street level, then you don't have to dig as far down to get an eight-foot ceiling in the basement garage. Keep in mind, however, that you also have to allow for the additional height of the first-level floor joists, the thickness of the poured garage floor, and any other items in the ceiling of the garage that might require a higher ceiling, such as pipes or steel beams. A simple rise-over-run slope equation will tell you how much run of driveway will be needed to descend a given distance, but check with your local building codes to find out the maximum slope allowed for an underground garage driveway. You do not want your driveway so steep that you have to gun your car just to get up the hill.

Because of these factors, basement garages often have lower ceilings than traditional aboveground garages, which can cut into overhead storage space. Going out to your car will also require you to walk down the stairs to your basement every time you want to go to your car. Lastly, because you will be coming up a sloped driveway when you pull out, you want to make sure you have a clear field of vision so that you do not accidentally hit any pedestrians on the sidewalk. If you have the room for a long driveway that slopes gently, this should not be a problem. An underground garage was the first plan for our addition, but we just did not have the room for a comfortable downward slope, especially given the fact that the garage is located on a semi-busy street with a lot of vehicular and pedestrian traffic. It worked out well since our new garage has a twelve-foot ceiling, making it ideal for hanging bicycles and other items using an electronic hoist system.

Every garage floor should slope slightly toward the garage door to allow spilled liquids or runoff from rain or melting snow to drain and not pool on the floor, usually 1/4 inch to 1/8 inch per foot, but check your local building codes (www.yourcarcave.com 2020). The apron in front of the door should slope even more.

Garage Heaters

Whether you plan to use your garage as a workshop or not, a heated garage is a worthwhile investment in comfort. If you have living space above or next to an attached garage, a heated garage provides an extra layer of protection against a source of cold air.

Electric garage heaters are the easiest to install, especially in detached garages where gas or hot water lines probably do not exist. These electric heaters cost more money to run than gas or hydronic heaters and might require a 220-volt outlet, so plan for this if you decide to go electric.

Gas heaters are very common in garages. They work very well and are ideal for large spaces, but they are not cheap—typically around $1,000 for a small one. They also require a dedicated gas line and venting out the side wall or through the roof. This was a deal-breaker for us. Our new attached garage was right on the lot line, so we could not install any venting out the side of the garage, and with living space above, venting through the roof would have been problematic. We therefore decided to go with a hydronic hot water heater connected to our new radiant floor heating system. Hot water from the boiler is piped into the heater, where it is circulated through coils. A fan blows air over the hot coils, creating warm air that is blown throughout the garage. It has its own thermostat, and installing this type of unit was as simple as running the PEX hot water tubing to the unit with the rest of the radiant heating system; no venting was necessary. The hydronic system is very efficient and safe. I keep the thermostat set to 55 degrees all winter unless I will be working in the garage; then I turn it up.

Whatever type of heating unit you choose, make sure it is sized properly. Electric units are usually rated by wattage and square footage. Gas and hydronic systems are rated according to their BTU output, so have your HVAC contractor determine the size unit needed for your garage.

Garages also need to be properly vented. Most detached garages have roof vents to circulate air and remove humidity, but proper venting is very important for attached garages since people often store hazardous chemicals in the garage, such as paint, lawn chemicals, and gasoline for yard equipment. Cars and gasoline will also off-gas benzene, which is a carcinogen. One way to mitigate these problems and improve the indoor air quality of homes with attached garages is to make sure your garage has a ventilation system (Mallach et al. 2016). There are a variety of ventilation fans available, but there are better ventilation systems designed specifically for garages. These systems can even be connected to certain garage door openers. When the garage door closes, the ventilation system will kick in for a preset amount of time and expel garage air and car exhaust to the outside. Most people are not aware of the hazards of benzene or other VOCs found in many garages, but more is finally being written about these issues. Check with your HVAC contractor for more information on garage venting fans and systems.

Other things you can do to improve the indoor air quality of homes with attached garages include making sure the door leading to your home from the garage is properly sealed, making sure your garage is insulated and drywalled with all joints sealed, and storing chemical products in an outdoor shed.

Garage Photographs

Figure 26. The orange cross-linked polyethylene pipes, better known as PEX tubing, circulate hot water through the garage heater from the boiler. The hot water is circulated through coils in the heater, and a fan blows the warm air throughout the garage. These hydronic heaters can be connected to their own thermostat and eliminate the need for a gas line and venting through the roof or wall as with gas heaters.

Figure 27. We lost the back door to the house and the easiest way into the basement from outside when we built the addition. The new back doors were in the kitchen and garage with no direct path to the basement. Knowing this would make it difficult to get large items into the basement without going through the house, we concealed a new staircase in the garage under these steps that go up to the kitchen. The stairs are powered by linear actuator motors that flip the stairs upward, revealing steps down to the new basement.

Figure 28. Picture of the stairs raised to reveal the steps going down. The linear actuators can be seen mounted under both sides of the stairs. Building codes require a concrete gas curb around the perimeter of garages in the event gas should spill out of a car. There is a gas curb around the entrance to the stairs going down to the new basement. We chose a custom pedestrian entry door for the garage that matched the Spanish-style look of the home. Check your local building code for gas curb requirements. If you are reading this on a Kindle click this link to see a video of me testing the moving staircase during construction:
https://www.youtube.com/watch?v=XyWxNUnaH6I&t=10s.

Figure 29. A motorized bicycle hoist by Garage Gator keeps bikes off the floor and hung above the car. At the push of a button, the bikes are lowered to the floor where they can be removed from the rack. This is an incredible space-saving device, but it requires a high ceiling in the garage to keep the bikes suspended over a tall car. This hoist system holds six bikes. We use a smaller hoist to keep our Christmas tree stored at ceiling height. The tree is stored in a large cargo bag then strapped to the hoist rack. The drainpipes for the new second-floor bathroom located above the garage can also be seen.

Figure 30. The bike hoist in the lowered position. The wall-mounted shop vac and wall-mounted air compressor connected to a fifty-foot hose reel are great conveniences that are easily stored out of the way. The hose reel makes it easy to fill car and bike tires with air. The length of the hose reel makes it possible to fill car tires while the car is still in the driveway. If you are reading this on a Kindle click this link to see a video of the working bike hoist:
https://www.youtube.com/watch?v=7uZ2Z3mDTrA.

Figure 31. A wall-mounted garage door opener can save valuable space for storage over a car. They also come with motion-activated lights that can be installed on the ceiling that go on automatically whenever a person enters the garage, or the garage door opens. These openers, along with high-lift rails, are a necessity when installing a car lift.

Figure 32. When garage space is at a premium, car lifts make it possible to park two cars in one spot. Taller vehicles require a higher ceiling, but car lifts also make it possible to store snow blowers, lawn tractors, ATVs and other large items off the floor. A single-post lift like this one retails for under $9,000, not including freight delivery and assembly. Four-post car lifts are substantially cheaper. Make sure power outlets and the poured concrete floor meet the minimum requirements as specified by the car lift manufacturer. The manufacturer will specify the required thickness of the garage floor, the PSI (pounds per square inch) rating, and whether the floor should be reinforced with rebar or wire mesh. Photograph provided by American Custom Lifts. Photograph used with permission.

Figure 33. A center platform can be installed to fill in the lift, creating a storage platform for large items if the lift is not being used to park a car. With proper planning, a lift system can solve your parking and storage needs, but be sure to plan for this ahead of time. Photograph provided by American Custom Lifts. Photograph used with permission.

Chapter 9
Foundation

If something is important enough, even if the odds are against you, you should still do it.

—Elon Musk

As previously mentioned, in new construction, underground utilities will have to be piped to the site and laid before the foundation is poured. These usually come into the house through the foundation slab if there is no basement. Otherwise, they are brought through the foundation walls, either through a sleeve placed in the walls as the foundation is poured or drilled through the new foundation and sealed with hydraulic cement before the foundation is waterproofed. Waterproofing should be done by a company that specializes in waterproofing foundations and will warranty their work. This can be very important when building an addition in which the new foundation meets the old foundation. The waterproofing company should fill the joints with an epoxy compound (Palmer and Newman 2020).

It is extremely important that the finished foundation is high enough over the soil to prevent water from spilling over the foundation sill into the basement or crawl space during heavy rains. Local building codes will stipulate how high above grade the foundation sill should sit, often four to six inches, but these are minimum guidelines, and some experts recommend the finished foundation sit two feet higher than the highest point of grade within ten feet of the foundation to allow soil to grade away from the foundation (Carter 2003).

> **Builder Alert: It is extremely important the finished foundation is high enough over the soil to prevent water from spilling over.**

Often, the same contractor will do the excavation and pour the footings and foundation walls. The area to be excavated should be clearly staked after all underground utilities have been located. Excavation contractors hire hauling companies with dump trucks to remove the excavated earth. The cost is usually computed based on the number of cubic yards of dirt that have to be removed and hauled away. We had no place to put all the excavated dirt, so for our project, it took about twenty large dump trucks lined up down the street and coming and going all day to remove the dirt. Excavators often sell the dirt they remove. It is your dirt, so if it is being sold by the excavator or trucking company, make sure you are getting paid for it.

If you are building wood framing on top of the sill (the top of the foundation walls), anchor bolts should be embedded in the concrete when it is poured. After the footings and walls are poured, complete any other underground sewer or utility work before the slab floor is poured. Gravel will be dumped at the bottom of the foundation, and concrete poured over that will serve as the foundation/basement floor. Dirt will then be backfilled against the foundation.

It can take twenty-eight days for concrete to fully harden, or cure. This is the safest time to start the next phase of building, though some builders start backfilling and building when the foundation is 50 percent cured. This usually takes about seven days (Allen n.d.). Colder temperatures can result in longer curing times, but check your local building codes and inspection requirements. The hydration process needed for curing virtually stops at temperatures at or below 40 degrees Fahrenheit (Palmer 2020). Driveways need about seven days before you can drive on them, though some contractors say to wait several days longer if you have a large vehicle or pickup truck (Taylor n.d.(a); Vila and Taylor n.d.).

Footings

The footings are the most important part of the foundation. Footings provide a wider base to support the foundation walls and provide an edge for the foundation slab floor. Your architect should specify the footing requirements, but a general rule of thumb is the width of the footings should be twice the thickness of the foundation walls, and the depth of the footings should be equal to the thickness of the foundation walls (Lester and McGuerty 2016, 162). The footings must be poured below the frost line to prevent shifting during freezing and thawing cycles (frost heave). Frost lines vary from one climate zone to another so check your local building codes.

> **Builder Alert:** Footing width should be twice the thickness of the foundation walls, and footing depth should be equal to the thickness of the foundation walls.

Control and Expansion Joints

Make sure your architect and masonry contractor include any necessary control and expansion joints. A control joint is a partial joint through a concrete slab or wall that helps control potential cracks that might develop. Expansion joints are vertical or horizontal joints used to control structural movement often caused by temperature changes, such as freezing and thawing cycles. Expansion joints are usually filled with a material such as backer rod and then sealed.

Make sure all concrete flat work is included in your bid, including the garage pad, driveway, sidewalks, et cetera. Make sure your concrete contractor knows he will be expected to come back and pour the driveway and sidewalks when all other construction is finished. Do not be afraid to hold back a portion of the payment until this part of the job is complete.

Drain Tile

As previously mentioned, drain tile is typically installed around the perimeter of the foundation near the footings to collect groundwater during rain. The drain tile, usually perforated four-inch diameter PVC, corrugated pipe, or clay tile, directs groundwater away from the foundation to prevent the buildup of hydrostatic water pressure that leads to cracks in the foundation and seepage. PVC or corrugated pipe is now widely preferred. The drain tile is installed over gravel with the holes pointed down to absorb the groundwater. The pipe should be sloped one inch for every twenty feet. The drain tile is then covered with an additional eight inches of gravel and landscape fabric to prevent dirt and silt from clay soil clogging the perforated holes (Lester and McGuerty 2016, 170). The drain tile directs water into a sump pit in the basement; a sump pump pumps the water into the sewer line where it flows into the municipal sewer system or out the side of the house.

Sewer Lines

Local building codes will stipulate the materials and process for connecting underground sewer and water lines. Cast-iron waste and sewer pipes are quieter than PVC materials (Carter 1995). In Chicago, cast-iron sewer pipes are connected with oakum (hemp impregnated with tar) and sealed with molten lead (check your building codes). Chicago uses a combined waste and storm sewer system. Other localities have separate sewer systems for waste and storm water.

Most homes have gravity-fed sewers, so the lowest plumbing fixture in a home or addition must still be above the sewer line. A slope of a quarter inch per foot of pipe is recommended for sewer lines to drain properly (Lester and McGuerty 2016, 214). Too much slope and the water will drain faster than the waste, leading to clogs. Too little slope and the waste will not drain.

Once the foundation has cured and been waterproofed and backfilled, you are ready to start framing or bricking.

Builder Alert: The lowest plumbing fixture in a home or addition must be above the sewer line. A slope of a quarter inch per foot of pipe is recommended for sewer lines to drain properly.

Foundation Photographs

Figure 34. A small excavator digs out the dirt where the original garage stood. The dirt went from the excavator to the ground, where it was immediately scooped up by a small tractor, which then deposited the dirt directly into the back of the dump trucks. After the dirt was removed, the foundation for the old garage was removed along with the sidewalk in the gangway that ran between the garage and the house. If you are using a Kindle click this link to watch a short video of the excavation:
https://www.youtube.com/watch?v=_FkozfCSROA

Figure 35. With all the dirt and concrete from the old garage removed, wood forms and rebar are installed to shape the footings of the new structure.

Figure 36. The foundation and footings of the existing home can be seen as the addition is excavated a foot lower than the existing basement. The previous garage floor slab and the sidewalk between the house and garage ran just below the glass block windows of the existing basement. The cut-through to the old basement will be where the glass block window is located to the left in the foreground.

Figure 37. This is the view from the north driveway. Everything in the foreground will be filled in for the new garage. The old back door to the house can be seen in the center with the backyard patio in the background.

Figure 38. The cement truck backs up to the site to begin pouring the footings.

Figure 39. The footings and foundation walls have been poured. Notice the drain tile around in the inside perimeter of the footings that direct water back to where the sump pit will be located, underneath the concealed stairs that will go to the new basement from the new garage. Like the old garage, the new structure is directly on the lot line so we could not install drain tile around the outside perimeter of the foundation. The new basement will be below ground in the area shown, with the new kitchen above and level with the existing first floor. The new garage will be located where the tractor is seen in the photo. The addition will be topped off with a new bedroom and master bath level with the existing second floor.

Figure 40. Cast-iron sewer pipes can be seen beneath the gravel base before the concrete slab is poured for the new basement floor. The pipe sticking up over my right shoulder will be the drain for the new kitchen sink. Most homes have gravity-fed sewers, so the lowest plumbing fixture in a home or addition must still be above the sewer line. A slope of a quarter inch per foot of pipe is recommended for sewer lines to drain properly (Lester and McGuerty 2016, 214). Too much slope and the water will drain faster than the waste, leading to clogs. Too little slope and the waste will not drain.

Figure 41. Dimpled plastic drainage boards can be seen in this picture of the new basement under the new kitchen. These plastic sheets are installed one inch off the foundation walls and direct any water that might enter the foundation down to the footings and into the drain tile leading to the sump pump. These drainage boards add another layer of protection from water entering the basement through any cracks that might develop in the foundation walls.

Chapter 10
Masonry and Framing

If you're not stubborn, you'll give up on experiments too soon. And if you're not flexible, you'll pound your head against the wall and you won't see a different solution to a problem you're trying to solve.

—Jeff Bezos

As previously mentioned, older homes were made out of structural brick with solid brick walls that supported the structure. Some additions and many commercial structures are built using concrete blocks, which are then covered with face brick. In these cases, the masonry work is completed after the foundation is poured. Since our rear addition was built right up to the property line with another home behind us, the building code required a three-hour fire-rated wall, so the entire new structure had to be built out of block and brick construction, with the wood framing on the inside. The extra masonry work drove up the cost, but the addition is as solid as the original home. Most brick homes today are built using face brick or a siding material over a house wrap such as Tyvek, which is installed from the bottom up, over the wood framing. In this case, rough framing comes after the foundation work. If the façade of your home will be built with siding or stucco, it will be applied after the structural framing is complete and must be accompanied by waterproofing materials, including a waterproof membrane, flashing, and sealants around doors and windows. These must be applied at the time the windows are installed and before the siding. Stucco homes require the use of sheathing and a metal lath, to which the plaster is applied, and the use of expansion joints to control cracking (Lester and McGuerty 2016, 237). Siding is the most economical exterior covering and is available in wood, fiberboard, fiber cement, vinyl, and aluminum (Lester and McGuerty 2016, 241). Stucco and siding have to be installed by different subcontractors, and all these materials have their own advantages and disadvantages.

Illinois Brick is a major supplier of masonry materials in the Chicagoland region, but definitely use the internet or ask people in the building trades to find masonry suppliers in your area. Newer brick is easier to match, but many masonry suppliers still carry brick to match older homers. If the brick you are looking for is hard to find, you might have to contact a company the deals in reclaimed antique bricks. These outfits, such as Colonial Brick Company located in the Pilsen neighborhood of Chicago, buy bricks from demolished old buildings and homes, clean them, and resell them.

Lintels and Angle Irons

Make sure your masonry contractor knows the color and thickness of the mortar joints you desire. Along with the type of brick you choose, these factors will greatly affect the look of your home, especially when building an addition where it is aesthetically important that the new masonry matches the existing masonry. Your masonry contractor will also purchase and install the lintels and angle irons needed to support the weight of the structure over door and window openings, as well as any limestone door and windowsills or decorative limestone accents. An angle iron is a type of lintel that holds bricks in place over door and window openings in masonry construction. The masonry or framing contractor will also have to install any structural steel beams.

In our addition, we had to purchase a steel angle iron header beam that was rolled at the factory to the radius we wanted for the arched opening over the garage door. We also had to order a longer, straight steel beam that carried the weight of the second floor of the addition. This beam was notched into the masonry of the existing home and the masonry of the new outside wall of the addition.

Large steel beams will come from a steel company, but the smaller lintels and angle irons for doors and windows will often be supplied by the brick supplier. Be sure the price of any and all lintels and angle irons are included in the bids from the brick suppliers. A representative from the brick supplier should be able to meet with you to go over brick choices for your project. Be sure to provide your brick supplier with a copy of your blueprints as bricks are usually sold by the pallet, and the cost is estimated based on the square footage of brick needed.

Weep Holes

Weep holes are small holes drilled into masonry walls with a small diameter rope (wick) sticking out (Beall 1991). Weep holes are located near the bottom of masonry walls every two feet on center or above the flashing of doors and windows to allow water to escape along the path of the wick (Taylor n.d.(a)). Make sure weep holes are not too close to the ground or decking where water can pool up and enter the masonry through the weep holes. Weep holes were not used in older construction but are often required now.

> **Builder Alert: Make sure weep holes are not too close to the ground or decking where water can pool up and enter the masonry through the weep holes.**

Control and Expansion Joints

Make sure your architect and masonry contractor include any necessary control and expansion joints. As previously mentioned, a control joint is a partial joint through a concrete slab or wall that helps control potential cracks. Expansion joints are vertical or horizontal joints in masonry used to control structural movement often caused by temperature changes, such as freezing and thawing cycles. Expansion joints are usually filled with a material like backer rod and sealed.

Framing

The rough framing subcontractor plays a crucial role, especially when building an addition. Their measurements, precision of work, and knowledge of rough framing are crucial components in a successful project. Your rough framer's measurements have to be exact when building an addition to make sure the new finished floor meets the existing finished floor, taking into account the thickness of floor joists, the subfloor, and finished floor materials.

The rough framing contractor will most likely order all the materials as needed for the job from their lumber supplier. Make sure you are getting their contractor discount. To make sure you are getting a good price, submit your blueprints to a few different lumber suppliers and ask them to perform a takeoff bid. They will comb over every aspect of the plans and generate a list of lumber materials according to your architect's specifications, from the wood studs to the sheathing for the roof.

Laminated veneer lumber (LVL) is a very strong engineered framing material common in construction. It is typically used for floor joists, headers, beams, and ledger beams, but it costs a good deal more than traditional wood framing pieces. Make sure the cost of any and all LVLs is included in your lumber bids.

Find out from your framing contractor if they are supplying the glue, nails, anchor bolts, joist fasteners, and all necessary materials or if you need to order them with the lumber. Do not pay for these items twice. With our project, Hilti anchor bolts were needed to secure the framing to the masonry walls. Be sure the cost of the bolts is included in your bids if needed. Your architect will specify the thickness of framed walls. Walls consisting of 2' x 4' studs, 16 inches on center (every 16 inches), have been the standard, but builders are using 2' x 6' framing more and more because the thicker walls allow for increased R-values for insulation and more room for certain types of piping.

Floor joists are typically installed either 12 inches or 16 inches apart on center, depending on the span, or length, of the joist, but your architect will specify the type and thickness of the joists based on the span and materials to be used. Joist hangers are now used to connect the joists to the perimeter framing or a horizontal ledger beam attached to the masonry with anchor bolts. Pockets cut into the masonry used to provide ledges, or pockets, for joists to fit into, but this is now against code in many locations because any moisture that might penetrate the masonry could erode the wood joists over time. Additionally, clay tile and slate roofs are very heavy, and the framing for these roofs has to be designed to accommodate the extra weight.

Three-quarter-inch plywood has been a standard for subfloors for many years, but tongue-and-groove oriented strand board (OSB) is becoming a common substitute (Lester and McGuerty 2016, 187). Make sure all subfloors are screwed and glued down. It is the sliding of the wood against the nails that makes floors squeak. Make sure all headers and firestops are included in the framing bid. Firestops are horizontal pieces of wood framing between the studs that prevent or slow down a potential fire climbing up through the walls.

The motor/canister for central vacuum systems is usually located in a basement, garage, or first floor laundry room. The hoses for these systems run between floors and walls so they have to be installed after the framing but before the drywall. There are pros and cons to these systems, and they can cost several thousand dollars. Research them before you decide on one.

Pocket Doors

Pocket doors are a great way to save space in tight places, but they require a lot of extra work and cost over traditional swing doors. Pocket door frames have to be built into the walls as part of the framing. You can buy pocket door kits at home centers and supply houses, but they require much more work to assemble, so there is added labor involved. Make sure all pocket door frames are included in your framing labor costs. Pocket door frame sizes and costs are determined by the size, thickness, and weight of the door. You can buy entire kits with the doors, but these are often not quality wood doors. We used solid wood doors I bought at a salvage house that matched the 1920s-era wood doors in the existing house. I found a forty-two-inch-wide Victorian pocket door for the wide opening from the new bedroom to the master closet area. I made sure each pocket door frame door met the size and weight requirements for each door. Whatever doors you use, make sure your pocket door frames and wall framing meet the needed measurements for all components. Also, be sure to take into account any plumbing or electrical piping that might get in the way of the doors when they slide into the wall. Since one of our pocket doors was to the new bathroom, we had to make sure the door cleared the sink plumbing.

> **Builder Alert: Make sure to your rough framer adds 2″ x 4″ blocking to the wall studs wherever you plan to hang heavy objects that will require something solid to nail or screw into, such as towel holders, toilet paper holders, shelves, heavy paintings, wall cabinets, et cetera. Measure and write down their locations so you can easily find them after the drywall is up, and you are ready to hang your items.**

Masonry and Framing Photographs

Figure 42. The concrete block forms the structure of the rear wall of the addition that will be covered with the reclaimed brick from the old garage to match the house.

Figure 43. The pedestrian door opening to the garage that will lead up to the new kitchen, has been bricked but not mortared yet.

Figure 44. The curved-angle iron beam being unloaded will carry the weight of the addition over the garage door and hold the arched design of the brick in place. Your architect or a structural engineer can calculate the specifications of any beams you might need.

Figure 45. The arched brickwork around the garage door opening has been completed with the rest of the garage façade. The garage door was arched to match the arched windows of the dining room on the same side of the existing house. A new patio over the front of the garage will be accessible from the new bathroom. The wall studding seen in the middle forms the wall that will separate the new kitchen from the garage.

Figure 46. The framing for the clay tile overhang is being built to replicate the tile overhangs that once stood over the doors on each end of the original garage. The window for the new bathroom above the garage was arched to match the arch of the garage door. To the right of the window is the door that leads out to the patio from the new bathroom.

Figure 47. The garage overhang has been finished with Spanish clay tile and copper flashing to match the tile roof of the existing home. Each end of the original garage had a tile overhang like this. Brick driveway pavers have been installed over a concrete slab to prevent the pavers from sinking. Brick pillars flank the entrance to the garage and the driveway on the other side of the house. The iron arch over the driveway had to be custom made to replace the original arch that had rusted and was taken down years earlier. The pattern was replicated from the arch over the other driveway. The hanging lanterns are on timers that go on automatically with the other outdoor lights. Be sure to use only driveway-grade pavers that will not crack under the weight of cars.

Figure 48. The framing of the new kitchen floor, which also serves as the ceiling for the new basement, is underway. The openings for the kitchen windows and door leading to the patio are in the background. Notice the iron lintels over the window and door openings and how they extend beyond the openings. Your architect will specify how much bearing, or space beyond the opening, lintels and beams should extend and rest on the supporting structure on either side of the openings.

Figure 49. This opening is where the concealed steps will be built going down to the new basement from the garage. The steps going up to the new kitchen will be built over this opening, where a door to the new kitchen will be located. Notice the gas curb, required by code, that surrounds the opening. The glass block window in the existing basement will be removed and filled with brick.

Figure 50. View from the new basement around the corner to the entrance to the new basement where the steps will come down from the garage. The sump pump will be located under the steps from the garage so it won't take up room in the new basement. A wall and security door will be built in the background, creating a hallway to separate the new basement from the steps leading down from the garage.

Figure 51. View from the new kitchen looking toward the new garage. Metal joist hangers were used to secure the floor joists to ledger beams anchored into the masonry that run around the perimeter of the new structure for the first and second floors. LVLs were used as ceiling/floor joists twelve inches on center in the background to the support the wider span over the garage area while regular floor joists sixteen inches on center were used for the shorter span over the rest of the new kitchen.

Figure 52. Seen here is the ledger beam anchored to the outside wall of the addition and the floor joists of the new kitchen attached to the ledger beam with joist hangers.

Figure 53. Pocket door slid into its frame before drywall. This is a large, 1890s Victorian pocket door I found and used because it was wide enough for the forty-two-inch opening that separates the new bedroom from the new closet area and bathroom. The doors to the new bedroom, bathroom, and water closet match the doors on the existing home. Notice the double header over the door framing.

Figure 54. The masonry work for the south end of the addition is seen here from the backyard patio, along with the new kitchen door and window openings.

Figure 55. The addition where the tandem garage once stood meets the existing home just to the left of the gutter downspout. Mortar has been applied to the first-floor brickwork, and interior framing has been added for the windows for the new bedroom above the kitchen. Notice the double header over the window framing.

Figure 56. First- and second-floor brickwork has been completed and new bedroom windows installed. New crank-out casement windows have yet to be installed in the kitchen. A tile overhang is also being built over the kitchen door. I salvaged the beautiful oak door with a large window from an 1890s home that was being demolished. The door sat in storage for years. Notice the "soldier course" of bricks that make up the new windowsills. These match the sills of the existing home.

Figure 57. Most new structures have concrete steps that are poured with the foundation and surrounded with brickwork that matches the house. The patio drain runs under this area, so we could not excavate down to have a footing poured for the steps; we had to build wood steps. We used Trex composite wood decking, which comes in a variety of nice colors. The new casement windows for the kitchen, which match the French windows of the breakfast room on the other side of the home, have been installed. A screen door was also added.

Figure 58. The southern view of the addition seen from the outside with the Spanish clay tile gable roof that was extended over the new kitchen and bedroom.

Chapter 11
Roofing

*I fear failure, but I won't let it stop me. Sometimes you just
got to do it or else it just doesn't happen.*

—Mark Cuban

After your carpenter completes the rough framing and sheathing of the
roof, it will be time for your roofing subcontractor to install the roofing
materials, gutters, downspouts, and any fascia and soffits. The good
news is that there are plenty of roofing companies, so it should be easy
to obtain bids for your project.

Most homes have shingled roofs. Roof shingles are relatively
inexpensive, are easy to buy and install, and come in a variety of colors.
Many companies also offer "architectural" lines of shingles for a more
distinct look. Clay tile and slate roofs are beautiful and will last a lifetime
while adding an architectural flair to any home. While tile is common
with new homes in Florida and the Southwest, tile and slate roofs were
also used in many historic homes built across the country in the 1920s.
Unfortunately, they are extremely expensive to install because of the
cost of the materials and the labor involved in cutting and setting the tile
or slate. However, if properly maintained, these roofs can last fifty to a
hundred years and are impervious to rot, insects, salt air, and fire (Vila
n.d.). In fact, the underlayment, sheathing, and flashing will probably
have to be repaired long before the tile or slate.

If you are installing a tile or slate roof, it is extremely important that
you hire a roofing contractor who specializes in these roofs; there are not
as many of these companies around in colder climates, and they are not
cheap, but most roofing companies do not have the know-how to install
these roofs properly. It is also extremely important to make sure the
framing of your roof is designed to carry the extra weight of tile or slate.

**Builder Alert: Tile and slate roofs are very heavy. The framing
for these roofs has to be designed to accommodate the extra
weight.**

We were able to continue the clay tile gable roof over part of our addition, but we also had to incorporate a flat roof into the design. Flat roofs are easy to install but are also prone to water infiltration since the water does not flow off the roof. Flat roofs are often surrounded by a parapet wall. The framing of flat roofs has to be pitched just enough to allow water to flow toward a gutter or roof drain. Openings in the parapet walls allow water to flow through into scupper drains that channel it to gutters and downspouts. Some flat roofs have drains that channel water down interior piping into the sewer system. Roofers also use roofing "crickets" to direct water around obstacles such as chimneys or air-conditioning units toward the drains. Crickets can be prefabricated or built up under the roofing material with plywood or roofing insulation.

There are three basic options for flat roofing materials: modified bitumen, which is made from a rolled asphalt material that is torched down; rubber membrane, or ethylene propylene diene monomer (EPDM); and hot tar and gravel (Alexander n.d.). Other flat roofing options include polyvinyl chloride and vinyl (PVC) and thermoplastic polyolefin (TPO) (Roofing Calculator 2020). Each of these options have their pros and cons and vary in price. If building a flat roof, consult with your architect and roofing contractor to see which option is best for your home.

Flashing is used where a roof meets a wall, chimney, another part of the roof, or another object. Improper flashing is the cause of many roofing problems and leaks. Vent stacks will have to be installed for attic venting, bathroom fans, plumbing vents, and possibly fireplace and furnace exhaust vents. If these vents are not in place when the roof is installed, the roofer will have to come back to cut a hole, flash, and repair the roof where the vents are located. If your home has an attic, it is very important that it is vented properly so that air can circulate and moisture buildup is reduced. Depending on the design of your home, your attic might have gable vents, vents under the eaves, various roof vents, or ridge vents that run along the top of the roofline. Your roofer is responsible for installing these. Gable vents should be incorporated into the structure by your rough framer, mason, or siding contractor.

Whichever kind of roof you choose, make sure your roofer installs a quality felt underlayment over the roof decking and under the shingles or other roofing material. Also, make sure to use an ice and water shield on low-sloping areas of the roof. Many roofers are now using an ice and water shield as the standard underlayment for the entire roof because of its superior quality to regular roofing felt. The ice and water shield also seals itself around the roofing nails. In the long run, the ice and water shield might be worth the extra money for the entire roof, but make sure you know what materials your roofer is using as well as the cost of the materials.

Roofing Photos

Figure 59. The Spanish clay tile gable on the rear of the home was extended over the south end of the addition, matching the Spanish tile on the existing home. The new copper gutter was connected to the existing copper downspout.

Figure 60. A modified bitumen flat roof was used on a portion of the addition; otherwise, the entire existing roof would have had to been removed and reframed. Existing rows of clay tile were removed when the new roof was framed. The large round vent in the foreground is a bathroom vent fan. The smaller pipes are the vent stacks for the plumbing. The tall pipe in the background is the exhaust pipe for the new gas fireplace in the kitchen. Check your local building codes and the fireplace manufacturer's recommendations. Fireplace exhaust vents have to stick up high enough through the roof and be located far enough away to clear any obstructions or window and door openings when coming through a wall.

Figure 61. The parapet wall of the bathroom patio pictured here is similar to the parapet wall around the larger flat roof. However, this one has a limestone cap to accommodate the custom ironwork. Notice how the flat roof membrane is built up around the wall about a foot with a strip of metal counterflashing. The counterflashing is also caulked on top to prevent water penetration. Our building codes require balcony railings to be forty-two inches high. The wall height was designed knowing it would be capped with a railing to bring the total height to forty-two inches. Decking and wood deck roof squares can be installed over flat roofs to create a nice patio on balconies and rooftops.

Figure 62. Photo of the counterflashing and a roof drain. Since we are directly on the lot line, we had to use interior roof drains as we could not have gutters and downspouts on the outside wall that would have been on the neighbor's property.

Chapter 12
Heating and Air Conditioning

I think goals should never be easy, they should force you to work, even if they are uncomfortable at the time.

—Michael Phelps

Your heating, ventilation, and air conditioning (HVAC) contractor should be the next tradesman in line. Some general contractors bring in the plumber next after everything is under roof. This is optional, but plumbers and electricians have an easier time working around ductwork, whereas HVAC contractors are limited in where they can run ductwork. Having working heat and air conditioning also creates a more comfortable environment for the subsequent tradesmen to work, though your plumber and electrician will have to coordinate with your HVAC contractor to make sure the gas and electric are piped to where the furnace, air handler, and outside air-conditioning condenser will be located.

Your HVAC contractor will also install your kitchen exhaust ductwork and vents through the wall or up through the roof if needed. (Your kitchen cabinet installer should still be responsible for installing the vent fan unit you purchased with your cabinets and should connect it to the exhaust ductwork installed by your HVAC contractor.)

Central Heating and Air-Conditioning Systems

The majority of new homes and additions are still built with a central air- conditioning and heating system, also known as a forced-air system. These systems are relatively inexpensive compared to other systems and are serviceable by most heating and air-conditioning companies. These systems have the benefit of using the same return and supply ductwork for both heat and air conditioning, and all the components are relatively common. With central heating and air-conditioning systems, you can install air purifiers and humidification systems that serve the entire house.

That being said, I would not recommend a forced-air system if you can afford another option. The ductwork needs to be insulated and sealed properly, but it can still be prone to gaps that leak air and let dust into the ductwork, which gets blown throughout the house all year long. (The ducts should be cleaned to remove dust buildup every few years.) The warm air from these systems is also very dry unless the system is connected to a humidifier. The ductwork layout also has to be planned out ahead of time; the main supply and return trunk ducts can take up a lot of ceiling and wall space and often require soffits to conceal them. Forced-air systems are also not that efficient for two reasons. Once they cycle off, the house often starts feeling cold or drafty right away, leading some people to keep them turned up. Also, the same vents are used for hot and cold air. If the supply vents are near the floor, they are more efficient for heat since hot air rises but less efficient for the air conditioning since cold air is heavier and drops, making the ceiling the ideal location for air-conditioning vents.

When building an addition, you could also loss valuable space due to the ductwork when you just spent a fortune to increase the size of your home. Since our addition was limited to the size and shape of the existing garage we tore down, a forced-air system would have pretty much ruined it. We would have had to locate the new furnace and air-conditioning unit in the new basement, right under the kitchen. This would have taken up a huge chunk of space in the new basement, which we wanted to use as a finished exercise and hobby room. The supply and return ductwork would also have had to run directly up through the kitchen, interfering with the placement of the cabinets and the overall layout. We thought about installing a roof unit, but they are known to be noisy and to vibrate, and it would have to have been installed directly above the new bedroom. They also require a deep pocket to bring the ductwork down from the roof into the house, possibly eating up ceiling space unless we designed a higher roofline. The only choice that made any sense was to install a hot water radiant floor heating system and separate small-duct high-velocity air-conditioning system.

Radiators

To most people who did not grow up in a home with steam or hot water radiators, they might seem like unsightly clumps of metal that take up a lot of room. To others, radiators are a fantastic source of heat, although in small houses they can be in some inconvenient places. In fact, many homes and apartments built in the 1920s, after the Spanish Flu pandemic of 1918 and 1919, were designed with oversized radiators that would keep a residence warm even with the windows open (Sisson 2020). The Fresh Air Movement of the 1920s emphasized fresh air as an important means of fighting infectious diseases. Ironically, a hundred years later in the midst of the current COVID-19 pandemic, there is a renewed emphasis on ventilation, fresh air, and properly functioning windows to mitigate the spread of the virus.

A lot of house flippers and home remodelers have spent the last couple of decades removing radiators and their hot-water boilers in favor of installing forced-air systems. With sleeker European-style products, radiators are now making a comeback because homeowners are starting to realize their many benefits. These new wall panel radiators provide an even source of radiant heat that heats objects in the room, like the comfortable warmth of the sun heats objects, not just the air as with forced-air systems. When the boiler cycles off, the room still stays warm. Though the new metal radiators work well, they do not retain heat as well as the old cast-iron radiators (Think of the difference between cooking on a cast-iron skillet and in a conventional metal frying pan. The cast-iron skillet stays warm long after the heat is turned off.) Still, new flat panel radiators are being used more and more now, though it is expensive to build an entire house with radiators.

Radiant Floor Heat

Another highly efficient and even better option is hot water radiant floor heat. In fact, radiant floor heat dates back to the ancient Greeks and Romans. Radiant floor heat has all the benefits of radiant heat associated with hot-water radiators but does not take up wall space, is more efficient, and can also serve a variety of applications. New radiant floor heat is not like the radiant floor heating in some homes from the 1950s, which used copper tubing that often leaked, or the mesh electrical pads sold today, which will slightly warm a tile floor in the bathroom but do nothing to warm the entire room.

As with the new and old radiators, a boiler heats water, which is then circulated through tubing under the floor to heat the house. Like radiators, radiant floor heating systems provide even radiant heat without blowing dust everywhere or taking up valuable space with ductwork. However, these systems are not cheap and must be installed by an HVAC contractor experienced with them. I was somewhat surprised how few companies install these as they are becoming more common.

The components and labor drive up the price of radiant floor systems, but the main reason radiators and radiant floor heat are so much more expensive than traditional central air is that with central air, the heating and AC are installed together and use the same ductwork. You can spend the same amount of money installing a radiant heating system as a central air system, but you then have to install a separate cooling system, which can double the price. In fact, for a forced-air heating and cooling system for our addition, we were originally quoted a price of just under $10,000. That price included the HVAC contractor fabricating and installing all the supply and return ductwork as with any similar project. The cost of our radiant heating and separate AC systems came to twice as much—slightly more when we added the hydronic garage heater, an $1,800 unit that is fed from the same boiler as the radiant floor heat.

Installing radiant heat is not cheap, but if you can afford it, it is well worth the money, and nothing beats the feel of a warm floor beneath your feet. It is extremely efficient as the entire floor becomes one big radiator. On the coldest days, we only have to turn the heat up slightly in the addition for the rooms to heat up. Radiant heat does not make the air as dry as forced-air systems do and has the added benefit of being able to feed hydronic towel warmers, like we installed in the new bathroom; baseboard heaters, like we installed in the new basement; a hydronic garage heater; and ice-melting systems installed under sidewalks and driveways (a must for underground garages in cold climates). In short, this is the best source of heat and is also adaptable to a variety of uses and applications. And we lost no room in the new basement for a furnace or in the kitchen for ductwork.

With hot-water radiators, boilers heat water to 180 degrees Fahrenheit and circulate it through metal pipes that feed radiators throughout the house. Hot-water radiant floor heat uses water heated to 120 degrees Fahrenheit and circulated through rigid but somewhat flexible plastic pipes, like cross-linked polyethylene (PEX) tubing. The water is pumped to a manifold and then distributed to the entire house via a system of zones and subcircuits within the zones. Each room can be its own zone and have its own thermostat for individualized comfort and efficiency. Unfortunately, you cannot run radiant floor heat off an existing hot-water radiator boiler because of the temperature difference.

The only way to do this would be to run water from the existing boiler to a separate mixing tank, where it would be mixed with cold water and cooled to 120 degrees. Once the water returns, it would have to be heated back up to 180 degrees before reentering to the boiler. Failure to do this would lead to thermal shock and ruin your boiler. It is easier to purchase a separate boiler.

Boilers for radiant floor heating systems are not that big and can hang on a wall. We hung ours in the existing boiler room with some of the piping for the system. PEX tubing takes the water for the five zones we created (new kitchen, new bedroom, new bathroom, garage heater, and baseboard heat in the new basement) to a manifold in the wall of the new basement, then up to the proper rooms. No space was lost at all.

Radiant heat and the PEX tubing can be installed in a number of ways. It can be installed in the ground with concrete poured directly over it, making it ideal for basements, sidewalks, and driveways. The PEX tubing can be installed underneath subflooring from the room below using the "staple-up" method, in which the PEX is snapped into metal heat transfer plates between the ceiling/floor joists (make sure to get transfer plates in the proper width to fit twelve-inch- or sixteen-inch-wide joists) and then covered with a thin blanket of reflective material to direct the heat upward through the floor. Or it can be installed in floor panels directly under the finished floor, where the PEX tubing snaps into premade grooves in the floor panels. This is the most efficient method of installing radiant floor heat because the heat does not have to travel up through a subfloor then through another layer of finished floor to heat the room above. The floor panels are also designed to radiate the heat farther upward. Radiant heat can also be installed in walls and ceilings, which could be quite useful in spa areas.

Several companies make floor panels that accept PEX tubing, either out of plywood or other materials that better reflect and radiate the heat upward or outward. Warmboard, Inc. is a company that specializes in radiant floor panels, and they make both structural flooring panels that can take the place of traditional plywood subflooring in the rough framing process and panels that can be installed over a subfloor or in walls. Despite their increased efficiency, these flooring panels add quite a bit of cost to the project over the staple-up method and have to be planned for ahead of time as adding an additional layer of subflooring over an existing floor can create floor height issues, especially in a retrofit project. If you are starting from scratch on a gut remodel, new home, or addition, the panels can be the better option if you can afford the added cost. Otherwise, installing the PEX tubing underneath the subfloor from the room below will save you from having to tear up the existing finished floor in a remodel and pull up all the wood trim and cabinetry and shave the bottoms of doors to accommodate the panel subfloor. If you have a basement with an unfinished ceiling, retrofitting at least your first floor using the staple-up method is easy, but retrofitting the second floor would, of course, require tearing out the ceiling of the first floor. Adding subfloor paneling to an existing floor can also throw off the height of the first step of a staircase or lead to uneven floors if one room has the new radiant heat but the adjoining room does not, so plan for the method that suits your situation the best.

You can install radiant floor heat under different kinds of floors; it is not recommended for use under carpeting. Some contractors and flooring stores recommend that it not be installed under wood floors unless they are engineered floors designed especially for use with radiant heating. This is because wood expands and contracts in different temperatures, and heating the floor can dry out the wood and cause it to crack or expand and contract too much. If you use engineered wood floors, make sure to purchase the kind for use with radiant heat because if something goes wrong with your floors, you could void the warranty if the manufacture warned against it. Tile floors work the best with radiant heat because tile will not expand or contract with fluctuations in temperature. Tile is also more efficient because it acts as a conductor of heat rather than an insulator. Still, tile is best used in bathrooms and kitchens, and most people do not want tile in bedrooms.

Wood floors are becoming increasingly popular in kitchens, where they add a warm look and are softer to stand on all day than ceramic tile. We wanted wood floors in our new bedroom and the new kitchen. Since we wanted to match the color of our existing oak floors, engineered wood floors were not an option. Our HVAC contractor assured us there would be no problem using traditional oak flooring. He also used the staple-up method, installing the PEX tubing under the new subfloors. After three years, everything has worked out quite well, including the wood floors, and the addition is toasty warm, even on the coldest "polar vortex" days. However, your wood flooring installer must be cognizant of the PEX tubing under the floor. We instructed our installer to use the shortest nails possible when installing the finished floor, long enough to go through the three-quarter-inch finished floor and the three-quarter-inch plywood subfloor but not penetrate the PEX tubing below. We had him experiment beforehand to determine the shortest nails he could use safely. We also had him leave plenty of space around the edges of the room to allow the wood floors to expand and contract.

> **Builder Alert: Your wood flooring installer must be cognizant of the PEX tubing under the floor. We instructed our installer to use the shortest nails possible when installing the floor. We also had him leave plenty of space around the edges of the room to allow the wood floors to expand and contract.**

Small-Duct High-Velocity Air Conditioning

Small-duct high-velocity central air-conditioning systems, such as the ones made by SpacePak and Unico, have become standard in old and historic home retrofit projects and have been featured on shows such as *This Old House*.

These systems do not use large ductwork like standard central air and heating systems use. Instead, they use pre-insulated two-inch flexible ducts that can be snaked through walls, around corners, down through ceilings, up through floors, and between floor joists to run from room to room and between floors, often without having to crack open walls or build large soffits. This is a great feature when trying to save old plaster walls and avoid building soffits everywhere to conceal ductwork. SpacePak and Unico claim their systems remove 30 percent more humidity than traditional central air-conditioning systems. They operate on the principle of aspiration, which uses air streams to mix air in a room to provide draft-free comfort (SpacePak n.d.). What's more, there is only one return duct used with these systems, which is often located in a central location, such as a hallway. As with a conventional central air system, the air handler can be located in an attic with the condensing unit outside, and these systems make the perfect partner for a hot-water radiator or radiant floor heating system in new construction, an addition, or a remodel.

My parents had a SpacePak system installed in the home over thirty years ago, though they only planned for it to cool the bedrooms on the second floor and two rooms on the first floor where they spent the most time. Surprisingly, however, many homeowners are still not familiar with these types of systems, many home improvement books do not mention them, and many HVAC contractors do not install them.

When we initially moved in, the system was not working anymore. We also wanted to cool the entire house, including the new addition, so we installed a five-ton unit that could do so. Running the ducts to the rest of the existing home and to the addition was not that hard. The flexible ducts are connected to outlets in the walls, ceilings, or floors of a house. Generally speaking, each ton of cooling can supply six to eight outlets, so our five-ton unit supplies over forty outlets throughout the house. A specific installation formula is used to determine the size of the unit and the number of outlets. The formula also takes into account the length of the duct runs. Different layouts of the main supply plenum are also recommended, depending on the needs of the home. Only use HVAC contractors who are certified SpacePak or Unico installers. These systems do not work like regular forced-air systems.

Mini-Split Air Conditioners

Another option for cooling specific rooms, especially large open spaces such as basements, garages, workshops, and attics, are so-called mini-split systems. They are a cross between window units and central air systems. These systems use a condenser unit located outside that runs a line set of electricity and coolant to a head unit located in individual areas of the home. Some condenser units can run up to four individual head units. Head units come in different sizes for different-size rooms. These units are relatively quiet, unlike regular window units, and cool large spaces quite well. They are best suited for mounting on outside walls, but they can be mounted on inside walls as well. Mounting mini-split units on an inside wall will require concealing the line sets that run outside somewhere in a soffit. This might also require a pump that pushes the condensation (residual water air conditioners produce) along a plastic drain tube and out of the house with the rest of the line set. If mounted on an outside wall, the drain tube runs out the wall and drips like a regular window air conditioner, but that will not work when it's mounted to an inside wall unless the drain tube can be pitched downward all the way out of the house. These units come with remote controls, and some have a dehumidifier feature and even a heating feature if connected to a heat pump, although most heat pumps are not that effective when temperatures drop below freezing.

Whatever heating and air-conditioning systems you decide on, make sure your HVAC contractor performs a heat-loss calculation for your home to determine what size heating and air-conditioning system you need. Heating systems are sized according to the number of British Thermal Units (BTUs) needed to heat a certain size space, and air-conditioning systems are sized according to tonnage. A proper heat-loss calculation will take into account square footage and the number of doors and windows, which are sources of heat gain and loss. If your HVAC system is not sized properly, it will not work properly. If your air-conditioning system is too small, it will not cool the house. If it is too big, your house can get clammy, and windows will fog up with condensation as the system will not adequately remove humidity from the home.

It is also important to remember that ductwork and central air and heating systems should not be located in or pass through garage space. (This is against code in many locations.) Any vents or ductwork in a garage can deliver toxic air and exhaust fumes to the main living space. Some municipalities allow ductwork in the garage if the ducts are properly sealed, insulated, and covered with drywall, but there is no way I think this is worth the risk when you consider all the paint, gasoline, cleaning solutions, and pesticides often stored in garages, along with the potential off-gassing of benzene from exhaust and gasoline sitting in the tank of a car.

HVAC contractors should also know not to locate return ducts for central heating and air-conditioning systems in bathrooms or kitchens where odor from these rooms can be picked up and circulated throughout the house.

HVAC Photos

Figure 63. The compact, high-efficiency boiler for the radiant heating system hangs on the wall in the boiler room next to the main house boiler. This boiler takes up very little room and vents out the wall of the house.

Figure 64. The boiler heats water that flows into this system of copper piping, and pumps carry the water to a manifold, where it is distributed to the radiant heating tubes under the floors. Each pump on the wall represents a different zone that is independently controlled with its own thermostat.

Figure 65. This is the radiant floor heat manifold with larger PEX tubing for supply and return runs to and from the boiler. The smaller tubes carry the hot water for the individual rooms. The manifold system was built right into the wall and covered with plexiglass, so it does not take up any room, but the valves are easily read.

Figure 66. In the "staple up" method, the PEX tubing snaps into grooves on the sides of the metal heat transfer plates, which are mounted between the floor joists, then covered with a reflective blanket that directs heat upward toward the room above.

Figure 67. Pictured here are Warmboard-S structural subfloor panels that have grooves designed to accommodate PEX tubing. The Warmboard-S panels install directly over floor joists, eliminating the need for plywood subfloors. Photograph courtesy of Warmboard, Inc. Photo used with permission.

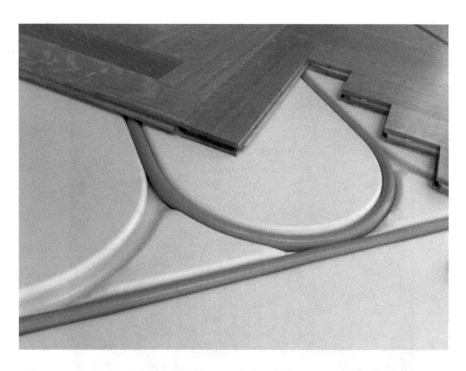

Figure 68. The Warmboard-R panels install over a subfloor and have built-in grooves to accommodate PEX tubing. Photograph courtesy of Warmboard, Inc. Photo used with permission.

Figure 69. This bedroom radiator was located in front of the window where we needed to cut through to the new bedroom in the addition. You can see boxes stacked up in the unfinished addition on the other side of the window. The radiator would have to be moved.

Figure 70. The same view shows the radiator removed and replaced by a cast-iron baseboard radiator that fits snugly against the wall. The window has been removed and a doorway cut through to the new bedroom with hardwood floors and wood trim matching the existing home.

Figure 71. These are four individual two-inch insulated flexible ducts for the SpacePak air-conditioning system. These four ducts run down from the attic through this linen closet and will feed four individual outlets in the rooms below. Only a small portion of the shelves had to be cut out, leaving the rest of the closet intact and usable. The round, flexible ducts can be snaked through walls and between floor joists to serve rooms above or below.

Figure 72. The round SpacePak outlets that deliver cold air to the rooms, as seen in this photo, are only a few inches wide and, when painted the color of the ceiling or walls, are hardly noticeable. The number of outlets a room needs depends on its size and potential heat gain from windows and doors.

Figure 73. The head on the mini-split air-conditioning unit cools the entire open space of the basement play area and home theater, though it is only needed on very hot and humid summer days.

Chapter 13
Plumbing

If you want to live a happy life, tie it to a goal, not to people or things.

—Albert Einstein

After your heating and air-conditioning system is installed, it will be time for the rough plumbing. Plumbing contractors often base their plumbing bids on a fixed amount of money per plumbing fixture. For example, if the plumber charges $400 per fixture, and there are two toilets, two bathroom sinks, two showers, and one kitchen sink, the plumber will estimate the price to be $2,800. The cost should include all materials and labor to run all the water and waste lines. If a plumber quotes prices using this method, make sure you find out if this price includes installing the actual fixtures when needed or if that's a separate price. Other plumbers will charge based on the time and materials needed to complete the entire job. Always check your local building codes for acceptable materials and venting requirements. Copper water lines, PVC drain lines, and cast-iron sewer lines and toilet stacks are common materials. Make sure all supply and drain lines for specialty items such as steam shower generators and jacuzzi tubs are planned out ahead of time according to the manufacturer's specifications.

Many municipalities allow the use of PVC for toilet drains and stacks, but as previously mentioned, the extra money for cast-iron pipes will be worth it in the long run to mitigate noise since cast-iron waste and sewer pipes are quieter than PVC (Carter 1995). A quarter inch per foot of pipe slope is recommended for sewer lines to drain properly (Lester and McGuerty 2016, 214).

Lastly, make sure your waste and water lines are vented properly. Vents that extend up through the roof supply fresh air to the plumbing system and allow the system to maintain proper air pressure. This keeps sewer gases from entering the home and allows wastewater gas and odor to escape.

Figure 74. Pictured here is the rough plumbing for the double sink in the new bathroom. Copper lines bring in hot and cold water, and the PVC pipes serve as the drainpipes and the vent pipe that extends through the roof. The open pocket door that leads to the bathroom can be seen to the right of the plumbing. Careful measuring was needed to make sure the door would have enough room to slide open without hitting the piping in the bathroom wall.

Chapter 14
Electrical

A goal without a timeline is just a dream.
—Robert Herjavec

It is easier for an electrician to bend conduit piping around obstructions than for a plumber to run pipe, so the rough electrical work comes after the rough plumbing. The work of the electrician is straightforward, but proper planning will be needed to accommodate certain items. Make sure the electrician is aware of any outlets that need to be in certain locations and other potential requirements. For example, bathroom vent fans with heaters require their own dedicated circuits. A steam generator for a steam shower will probably require a 220-volt line on its own circuit. An outlet for the pump in a jacuzzi tub will have to be installed in the proper location. Make sure you discuss all these items ahead of time and that they are documented in the architect's blueprints.

Homes should have at least a 100-amp circuit breaker box as required by code, but 150- to 200-amp service is becoming more common, especially if your home will have a lot of electrical equipment (Lester and McGuerty 2016, 238). For our project, our electrician installed a circuit breaker subpanel in the addition that was fed from our main circuit breaker panel.

Your electrician should be aware of all codes in your location and the proper gauge wiring for various applications. Your electrician should also run any and all internet cables and cable TV or antenna wires and install smoke detectors, audio/visual cables for home theaters, doorbell wires, telephone lines, and home security and video surveillance wires.

Your electrician will also be the one installing your lighting fixtures. Can lights, which have become increasingly common in kitchens, bedrooms, and basements, have to be roughed in before the drywall is hung. Other fixtures, such as pendant task lighting over a kitchen island, under-cabinet lighting, wall sconces, and vanity lights next to or over mirrors in a bathroom, have to be planned out as well. When possible, buy the fixtures ahead of time or at least obtain the measurements so that you and your electrician can plan the layout for the electrical boxes and the location of the fixtures when they are installed during the electrical trim (finish phase).

Figure 75. The rough electrical work for the new bathroom can be seen in this photo. The box for the outlet above the sink can be seen in the middle, just above the PVC vent pipes, along with the box to power the vanity light above the mirror. After we purchased the mirror, it became clear we would have to raise the outlet box to install the light fixture above the mirror, which turned out to be larger than we first thought. Luckily, the walls were not up yet, so it was an easy fix.

Figure 76. Ground fault interrupter (GFI) outlets like this one are required by code anywhere an outlet might be exposed to water, such as in bathrooms, kitchens, and garages, as well as on the exterior of the house. If the sensor in the outlet detects water, the flow of current is interrupted, and an internal switch shuts down the outlet until it is reset with the reset switch, preventing a prolonged surge of electricity. If you are remodeling a very old house, use the opportunity to have your electrician replace as much of the old wiring as possible, especially if the home contains old cloth wiring. This wiring is a major fire hazard. If the wiring is in conduit piping, the electrician should be able to pull new wiring room by room without opening the walls. Old knob-and-tube wiring might require opening the walls and ceilings.

Figure 77. Outlets like this one with built-in USB ports are great to install over nightstands or in kitchens because the ports facilitate the charging of cell phones, smart watches, tablets, and other USB-powered devices.

Figure 78. Home automation has come a long way with the advancements in technology. There are now smartphone apps and devices to control many aspects of a home automatically or with the touch of a button. We have a large TV in the basement but still like to watch TV upstairs. However, we did not want a television ruining the formal look of the living room or blocking the view of the French doors we open in the summer. The answer was to conceal and automate the opening of a TV in this large "coffee table" ottoman I found that matched our décor.

Figure 79. A standard TV lift cabinet would still block the French doors so the challenge was finding the right style ottoman big enough for a television. I searched stores and the internet for months until I found one that look liked it would work and that I could take apart and would still be sturdy enough to hold a TV. I put hinges on the top, removed the drawers, installed the linear actuators and remote control, and re-enforced the frame. I was still able to mount a 42-inch television and put a DVD and DVR in the base. An infrared repeater can be used to control devices out of the line of sight of infrared remote controls. If you have a Kindle click this link to see a video of the TV opening and closing:
https://www.youtube.com/watch?v=Y6cNvZjLEbc.

Chapter 15
Insulation

*I know how it looks. But just start. Nothing is
insurmountable.*

—Lin-Manuel Miranda

One major difference between older homes and newer ones is the quality of the insulation. In fact, very old homes were not built with any insulation. The most common insulation in very old homes might be rock wool insulation put in the floors of an attic. Yet good insulation is one of the most important factors in keeping a home cool in the summer and warm in the winter and making it more energy efficient, thereby cutting down utility bills.

I did not realize the power of insulation until we insulated the attic roof of our 1920s Chicago bungalow. The house I grew up in and the bungalow, which we bought when we got married, were both solid brick homes built in the 1920s with no insulation. The bungalow had a wonderful walk-up attic, but it was always very hot and humid in the summer and cold and drafty in the winter. We could even feel the effects of poor insulation one the main level of the house even though the attic floor had previously been insulated. We installed fiberglass batt insulation to the underside of the attic roof as part of an energy-efficiency grant from the Historic Chicago Bungalow Initiative. The results were astounding. The insulation kept the entire home cooler by blocking the heat from the sun before it even entered the home through the roof, and the added insulation kept the heat from escaping the house through the roof in the winter. I was a believer, so when we started the addition on our current home, I knew I wanted it properly insulated.

There are many insulation products on the market. Insulation is rated according to R-value. R-value measures how well insulation can prevent the flow of heat in and out of a home (Home Depot n.d.). There are seven different climate zones in the United States as defined by the US Department of Energy. Each zone has a suggested R-value for insulating attics, walls, floors, and crawl spaces. Consult an R-value climate zone map for your location or an insulation contractor. Generally speaking, the greater the R-value, the better the insulation will perform.

Fiberglass batt insulation comes in rolls that are easily stapled to the studs between walls, ceilings, floors, and roof joists. Fiberglass batts work well and make for a great do-it-yourself job. However, other products have grown in popularity and work much better.

As previously mentioned, spray foam insulation has gained immense popularity with homeowners and builders in the last several years because of its high R-value and ability to get into tiny nooks and crannies, expand, and thereby seal off virtually any space where air loss or infiltration occurs. However, spray foam insulation is a cocktail of toxic chemicals that are mixed, often on site, to create the polyurethane foam. Isocyanates are chemicals such as methylene diphenyl diisocyanate (MDI), which are mixed with polyols that react to form the foam. When not cured properly, meaning not fully reacted, the chemicals can off-gas, or emit odors. The curing process can also produce other chemicals that contain VOCs. The Building Green website has a great article from 2011 (updated in 2018) that details the US Environmental Protection Agency's growing concerns about spray foam insulation, particularly when applied as a do-it-yourself job (Roberts 2011). See Badore (2018) for information on alternatives to spray foam insulation and Alter (2019) for other warnings from the Treehugger website.

Many general contractors now include this product as part of their bid because it has become so popular. Make sure you know what kind of insulation your general contractor uses and how much he is charging you for this product compared to other types of insulation. After researching all the pros and cons of spray foam insulation, I decided I would rather give up a little R-value and not have my house encased in a toxic envelope. Spray foam insulation is also more expensive than other types of insulation.

I decided on blown-in cellulose and was able to electronically submit my blueprints to an insulation company that provided me with a bid for the project. Once we were ready for insulation, the job only took two days: one day for the crew to staple all the mesh netting to the studs and joists that would hold the insulation in place and a second day to blow in the cellulose with their hoses. The cellulose can get into hard-to-reach places like foam insulation. The same insulation was used for soundproofing the walls between the floors and the interior walls of the new bathroom. The company also sprayed all the fireproofing foam required by code into all the vertical penetrations where pipes, electric conduit, or other openings run between floors. The results were fantastic. As soon as the insulation was complete, the building retained the cool air from the air conditioning, even without the drywall being up yet, and it blocked the noise from the semi-busy street where the home is located. Spray-in cellulose is also far cheaper than spray foam insulation. Cellulose is extremely green, made almost entirely out of recycled newspaper, is flame retardant, has a good R-value, is nontoxic, and works very well.

Take the time to do your own research on the various insulation options and talk to various companies that specialize in insulation. However, by choosing this method and choosing my own insulation contractor, I was able to save several thousand dollars off the cost of insulation as quoted in the bids I received for the addition from general contractors and wound up with a product that works very well and that I know is safe for my family.

Figure 80. The is the new kitchen once the cellulose insulation was installed. The wall to the left separates the kitchen from the new garage. All the walls were insulated, as well as the ceilings and floors for soundproofing.

Figure 81. This is the cellulose insulation applied to the walls and cathedral ceiling in the new bedroom.

Chapter 16
Drywall

It always seems impossible until it's done.
—Nelson Mandela

Having grown up in a 1920s-era home, I did not realize the greatness of solid plaster walls until I visited newer homes made out of drywall. The walls seemed thin and weak, and the entire wall would often move when leaned against. My disdain for drywall continued when we finished the basement in our Chicago bungalow. I framed the entire basement myself but left the drywall to someone else. I could not believe the mess from all the cutting, taping, and sanding. Nails for pictures could be pushed right in and pulled right out with just the force of one's hand, something that could never be done in a thick plaster wall. With plaster walls, the plaster is applied to and hardens over slats of wood lathe or wire mesh. Many of the older homes in the area, such as ours, even have pretty stucco designs swirled into the plaster, giving the home character. Unfortunately, plaster walls gave way to premade sheets of drywall decades ago.

At first, I wanted to plaster our addition to match the existing home, but it is hard to find plasterers these days, and when you do, the price can be quite high. I used a local plasterer to plaster the spaces where windows were removed for the addition. I wanted the spaces filled in with real plaster to match the plaster stucco of the walls. The plasterer did a fantastic job, but plastering the entire addition was more than he could do, and the company I found who could do it wanted to charge a great deal of money. When I considered that a lot of the addition was going to be a new kitchen, where the walls would be covered with cabinets, and a large new bathroom that was going to have a lot of wall tile, I figured it was not worth spending the extra money. If I was building a new house and money was not a factor, I would definitely have it plastered because the quality of the product is far superior to drywall. Another way to plaster that has been gaining in popularity is to hang wallboards made of blueboard and apply a coat of plaster over them. Drywall is covered with a layer of paper designed to absorb paint. Blueboard is designed to bond with a thin coat of plaster.

Contact a drywall contractor for a bid on your project. The contractor will need your blueprints or to see the jobsite. Drywall is sold in 4' x 8' and 4' x 12' sheets, though the 4' x 12' sheets are quite heavy. Check the price of materials in your bid against that of a drywall supplier. Have the supplier use the blueprints for an estimate of materials based on your square footage. Use the thicker 5/8" sheets of drywall and make sure your estimates include all the drywall screws, tape, and joint compound that will be needed. Based on the prices, determine if it is cheaper to have your contractor order all the materials from his supplier or for you to order them yourself. I ordered all the materials from a reputable drywall supplier who also had a boom truck that was able to lift all the sheets of drywall for the second floor up to the balcony off the new bathroom where there was a door. Otherwise, I would have had to pay a couple guys to carry all the sheets of drywall upstairs. Find out the terms of delivery from your drywall supplier. Is it curbside delivery only? Will they carry the drywall to where it needs to go? Will they carry the sheets of drywall upstairs? In short, in any situation, always ask what is not included in someone's price. My delivery included bringing the sheets of drywall where they were needed, but, as with a lot of other materials that were delivered, it was a lot of work, so I always made sure to tip the delivery guys well.

Pros can drywall an entire house in a few days. They make quick work out of cutting, hanging, and taping drywall. The residual mess can be overwhelming, so make sure cleanup is part of their job. Also, if your project is an addition, make sure all doorways to where the work is being done are covered with zip-down plastic coverings and cover all nearby objects. The dust travels everywhere. This is when a good cleaning crew comes in handy, especially if you are living in the house during this part of a renovation.

Wet areas that will be tiled, such as around bathtubs and shower walls, are not covered with drywall; they are covered with panels of concrete board, such as dura-rock, which are screwed into the studs. Tile can be applied directly to the dura-rock.

Builder Alert: Always ask what is not included in the price.

Figure 82. Drywall was delivered with a boom truck so the sheets could be lifted to the second floor and brought inside through a door leading to the patio off the new bathroom.

Figure 83. This is the breakfast room located off the old kitchen before the parquet floors were removed and the addition built. The room contained six French windows, but the ones to the right faced the old garage on the back of the house and had to be bricked up when the addition was built.

Figure 84. The back windows of the breakfast room were bricked up from the outside. Our plasterer was able to recreate the stucco design with real plaster where the windows were located to match the rest of the room. The antique Victorian fireplace mantle gave a us a place to put the cast iron door from another marble Victorian fireplace we already had. I put wood blocking in the window openings before they were plastered to give us something solid to screw into to mount the mantle. We put the marble fireplace in the new kitchen with a gas insert. The plasterer was also able to match yet a different stucco pattern in the original master bedroom where another window was bricked up.

Figure 85. Inside plaster wall of a bedroom that had to be removed because of mold and water damage from a leaky roof.

Figure 86. Same room after the wall was repaired.

Chapter 17
Flooring

Success consists of going from failure to failure without loss of enthusiasm.

—Winston Churchill

With so many flooring options available today, the choice of flooring materials often comes down to personal taste and price. It is hard to believe so many old homes were originally built with beautiful solid oak or maple floors that were subsequently covered when carpeting became a luxury item decades ago. Many homes built in the 1970s through the 1990s were built with carpeting over plywood subfloors. When more and more homeowners started pulling up their carpeting in recent years, the people who owned old homes had the advantage of having nice wood floors already there. Owners of more modern homes had to pay a lot of extra money to install new wood floors to replace carpeting.

More and more people are pulling out carpeting or avoiding it from the start because carpeting traps odors, dirt, and allergens such as dander and dust. While ceramic tile has been a staple in kitchens and bathrooms, more people are choosing wood floors in their kitchens because they are softer and therefore easier on the feet and knees than hard ceramic tile or even beautiful stone. Wood floors also offer a warmer look.

The internet and magazines are full of photographs of stunning kitchens and bathrooms that showcase all kinds of flooring materials, from marble, to stone, to wood, to ceramic tile, and other materials. Prestained and engineered wood comes in a variety of sizes and colors, and new vinyl and floating laminate floors can be good options for basements. (Definitely consider the new plank-looking vinyl flooring in basements prone to water.)

Radiant floor heat can also affect your flooring options. If you are using radiant floor heat, carpeting is not recommended. Engineered wood floors should be rated for use with radiant heat, or the warranty could be voided. Solid oak floors will work with radiant heat, and tile floors work the best.

When we renovated our current home, we found beautiful oak flooring that was still in good shape under the 1960s parquet flooring that had been installed over it in three of the main rooms in the house. The parquet was dark and outdated, and we liked the oak floors. The home had carpeting in the rest of the rooms, the hallways, and up a dramatic winding staircase. Much of the carpeting had been ruined by years of cat urine, as were some of the floors underneath. The good thing about wood flooring is that it can be refinished over and over again and easily repaired. After all the parquet and carpeting were removed, we refinished all the floors and replaced the wood that could not be saved. We wanted the existing house to flow into the addition, so we installed the same red oak flooring and stained it to match the existing floors. New engineered wood floors come prestained, but they often cannot be sanded and restained because they are made of thin veneer. Solid oak floors will last a lifetime and can be refinished many, many times.

If you are trying to match new wood floors for an addition, it might be hard to find new prestained wood floors in the same color, so you will have to buy unfinished floors and have your flooring contractor stain them the color you need. If you do buy prestained wood flooring, make sure it is the thicker kind you can sand and restain in the future; otherwise, if it wears out or gets damaged, you will have to tear up the whole floor if matching planks are no longer available. When you buy wood flooring, it is best to let it sit in the house for a few days to let it acclimate to the environment so that any expanding and contracting of the wood from temperature changes takes place before it is installed.

The expanding and contracting of wood is why ceramic tile cannot be laid directly over a plywood subfloor. The movement of the wood can cause the grout and tile to crack. A thin underlayment must be installed over the subfloor before the tile can be laid. Make sure your tile estimate includes the purchase and installation of the underlayment, the grout, the thin-set mortar, the tile spacers, and other materials needed for the job.

Builder Alert: Do not install tile flooring directly over a wood subfloor. You must install a proper underlayment first.

Floor Refinishing Photographs

Figure 87. First-floor hallway after the carpeting was removed. The floor in the back bedroom had to be completely replaced. The green cement floor by the step was the original floor in the sitting that been carpeted over.

Figure 88. The hallway turned out great after refinishing. Only a few planks of wood had to be replaced.

Figure 90. The dining room after the parquet floors were pulled up, revealing the original oak floors. The wiring for a floor buzzer that rang near the maid's room was still there. The iron gates match the railing on the main staircase. The arched French doors open into the room.

Figure 91. The dining room after renovation.

Figure 92. Originally the maid's room, the floor in this back bedroom had to be completely ripped up and replaced. Sleeper studs served as the subfloor over which the oak floors were laid.

Figure 93. The sitting room was originally an indoor/outdoor room with five French doors that opened into the room that had a green cement floor. We glued the new oak flooring to the cement floor and stained it to match the other refinished floors. The window awning blocks the southern sun in the summer but still allows us to open the doors and enjoy the fountain and flower garden outside.

Figure 94. Main staircase after the carpeting was removed. The dark 1960s parquet floor that was installed over the oak floors can still be seen in the rest of the living room. Countless hours were spent removing staples from the floors and stairs that were used to secure the carpeting and parquet flooring to the oak floors underneath. Use a nail puller or nail cutting pliers to remove the staples by rocking them back and forth rather than pulling them straight out with a regular pliers. It's much easier and could help avoid a case of carpal tunnel.

Figure 95. The parquet flooring has been pulled up and the living room floor and staircase refinished.

Figure 96. The upstairs hallway floor was in bad shape after the carpeting was removed, but only a couple planks of wood had to be replaced.

Figure 97. The upstairs hallway after refinishing the floors.

Chapter 18
Trim Carpentry

I have not failed. I've just found 10,000 ways that won't work.

—Thomas Edison

After your floors are installed, you are ready for the trim carpentry, including hanging the doors and installing the window and door casings and other moldings. However, your carpenter will have to return to install the baseboard trim around the cabinets in the kitchen and bathrooms. He will also have hang shelves in closets or install closet organizers after all the painting is finished.

Trim carpentry is a fine skill. Trim carpenters know all the technical terms such as "stool" and "backbend" that comprise windowsills and other casings. Your trim carpenter should measure the linear footage of all pieces of moldings, door jams, thresholds, baseboards, and casings that will be needed.

When deciding on trim, it is important that you first decide if you will want your trim painted or stained or if you want the option to do either. As previously mentioned, if you want to stain your wood trim, you will need to purchase trim in a quality stain-grain wood, such as oak. Pine is a harder, less porous wood that does not take stain well. Rather than absorb the stain, pine and other low-quality materials, such as medium-density fiberboard (MDF), which has no grain to it, keep stain from seeping into the wood, which is how stained wood achieves its deep, rich look. Those materials are better suited for painting.

Also, if you are building an addition, you have to decide if you want to match the woodwork. We had beautiful woodwork throughout the house, so I wanted to continue that in the addition. I also did not want the addition to look like an addition. I wanted the house to flow seamlessly from the old part to the new part, and I did not want to spend a fortune on the addition only to install cheap-looking molding.

Since most mill shops do not stock the style of woodwork from hundred-year-old homes, I had to find a mill shop that could replicate my woodwork. This required bringing in a sample of the woodwork I wanted replicated. The mill shop made a knife to match the contour of the molding and milled all the oak pieces to match. Depending on the mill shop, it might cost about $300 per knife (or molding) you want matched, in addition to the cost of the wood.

Figure 98. The baseboard trim in the addition matches the 1920s-era baseboard in the rest of the house. The extra cost for custom trim moldings might not be worth it for just one window or room, but the cost becomes negligible when buying trim for an entire home or addition, and you will have a truly custom look. We painted the bedroom trim and stained the trim in the kitchen. Other examples of the trim carpentry can be seen in the photographs of the kitchen.

Chapter 19
Kitchens

To win big, you sometimes have to take big risks.
—Bill Gates

Times have changed. Kitchens used to be small, utilitarian rooms in the back of the house or in the basement in much older homes. Now, kitchens are gathering places. New homes are often built with large kitchens. Many additions are built onto older homes to solve the problem of a small kitchen. Kitchens offer the biggest returns on investment homeowners can make.

Your kitchen will be determined by your needs, wants, space, and budget. Quality kitchen cabinets are made from a solid plywood box, not particle board. Make sure to ask about this. There are countless images of eye-popping kitchens on the internet and in magazines. Many are not realistic for the average person, either because of space or money. Still, it is good to see what designs and products you might like to incorporate into a new kitchen.

It is possible to spend countless hours on a kitchen design. Make sure your architect knows what you have in mind, and take your ideas with you to a kitchen design showroom. Big box stores like Lowe's and Home Depot offer free kitchen design services, as do many other places. The cost of cabinets can vary tremendously, so shop around and try to stick to a budget. That is sometimes not easy once you see all the new cabinets and built-in features available. The kitchen design representatives can be a tremendous help when designing a kitchen and picking out cabinets. Do not try to do this all in one day or in one store. Take your time, shop around, and synthesize all the various design ideas you come across.

We were limited in space with our new kitchen because of the size of our addition, but we doubled the kitchen space over the tiny first-floor serving area that had been used as the main kitchen for decades. The following photographs show the transformation from the old, small kitchen to the new kitchen in our addition.

Kitchen Photographs

Figure 99. For a small ten-foot-by-ten-foot room, the old kitchen turned out to be a lot of work. The wall where the windows are and where the sink was pulled out is where we will cut through to the new addition. The walls had multiple layers of tile and old wiring with a 1990s Pergo floor over a wood subfloor. In the new design, this room will be used as a serving and beverage station with a double refrigerator and extra cabinets.

Figure 100. After the windows and cabinets were removed, the masons started the work of cutting through the solid brick wall. The recently drywalled kitchen addition can be seen on the other side. The pipes for the old sink can be seen as they were encased in the middle of the brick wall and behind a layer of tile that was laid into cement over the brick.

Figure 101. The kitchen cut-through is complete. The pocket doors separating the old and new kitchens have been installed, along with the built-in butler's pantry on the opposite wall. The old pipes have not been removed yet and are still sticking up in the middle of the new threshold. I had removed the butler's pantry, two entry doors, and all the trim molding from a home that was being demolished nearby about fifteen years earlier and had always hoped to find a good use for them.

Figure 102. My parents had a beautiful Victorian marble fireplace mantle that had been in the basement for decades collecting dirt and moisture. I wanted to incorporate the fireplace into the addition, either as a functioning gas fireplace or as decorative piece, so I had it cleaned up and restored. I saved the cast-iron door and used it with a beautiful Victorian wood fireplace mantle I found at an antique store and installed them on the back of the old breakfast room wall where a bank of three windows had been removed when the addition was built. The marble surround wound up in the new kitchen with a Victorian-style gas insert.

Figure 103. I found this beautiful Victorian-style gas fireplace insert by Valor that I built the marble mantle around in the kitchen. Since the new kitchen is on the outside of the existing home, the area where an old window had been located was the perfect place for it. I had the masons cut the bottom of the window out down to the new floor and used the opening to recess the fireplace insert and exhaust venting so the fireplace would not stick out into the new kitchen too much.

Figure 104. I built the framing for the marble mantle, and the venting was run up through the walls and out the roof. Make sure to follow the installation instructions for a gas fireplace so as not to exceed the recommended number of bends or the distance for vent ducting. The SpacePak AC ducting for the kitchen can be seen sticking out of a small soffit to the left of the fireplace vent ducting near the ceiling.

Figure 105. The cut-through the to the new kitchen is complete and the opening trimmed out with woodwork matching the existing home. Oak floors matching the rest of the house were installed in the old and new kitchens, making for a seamless transition into the addition. The sink in the old kitchen was located in the middle of this new doorway.

Figure 106. There was not a lot of room in the new kitchen for a large refrigerator without ruining the flow. One wall of the old kitchen was a good location for a stand-alone refrigerator/freezer combo. The large, deep cabinets above are each six cubic feet (2' x 2' x 2') and can hold many large and small items. A hot-and-cold-water dispenser connected to the same water line as the freezer's ice maker sits next to the freezer on a fifteen-inch counter and supplies instant hot and cold water. Open cabinet shelving above is used for cookbooks and water cups. These Frigidaire units were only about $1,650 each compared to spending several thousand dollars each for Sub-Zero, Monogram, or Viking refrigerators. Those units are taller but also reduce storage space above.

Figure 107. Opposite the refrigerator is a serving station with a wine rack and cabinets with large drawers and pull-out shelves. The pull-out shelves are a great convenience—otherwise, the cabinets would require bending down and reaching back to get each item— and are well worth the extra money. Tall pantry towers are on the third wall of the room.

Figure 108. The main kitchen features quartz countertops and a marble tile backsplash to match the marble fireplace. Copper pendant lights provide task lighting above the island. A copper pot filler over the stove adds convenience. The cabinet next to the stove has a pull-out rack with step-back shelves designed to accommodate shorter and progressively taller pots. The microwave was mounted out of the way and built into the wall cabinets. The dark cabinets and matching range hood offer a contrast to the light-colored countertops and backsplash. Can lights throughout the kitchen offer plenty of lighting, as do the under-cabinet lights. The pot filler faucet is sixteen inches above the stove top, which is high enough to fill large pots. The minimum distance between an oven and an island should be forty-two inches.

Figure 109. The four-foot island offers a nice workspace without being too big for the kitchen and features an arched overhang that creates additional workspace without cutting into the walkway. Big islands are nice, but you don't want an island that is too big for the kitchen and interferes with traffic flow. This island contains a large silverware drawer, two deep drawers perfect for a lunch-making station, and a prep fridge to keep condiments, lunch meat, beverages, and other items handy.

Figure 110. The restored marble fireplace with a Victorian gas insert and simulated coals add instant warmth and a cozy feeling to the kitchen on cold winter mornings. The fireplace also serves as a beautiful eye piece and accentuates what would otherwise have been a plain wall.

Figure 111. A kitchen table sits in front of three casement windows that overlook the rear patio. The radiant floor heat keeps the kitchen warm even on the coldest days. We could have extended the cabinets and countertop and had a longer island, but we like sitting at the table by the windows rather than sitting on stools at an island.

Figure 112. The kitchen door and molding were reclaimed from the same house as the butler's pantry. The window lets in a lot of light, and the baseboard trim was custom milled to match the existing house and stained to match the door trim. A laundry chute built into the wall behind the door also serves the new bedroom above. A second laundry chute door was installed in the kitchen for dirty dish towels. The laundry chute empties into a wall cabinet in the new basement below, steps from the laundry room. Check your local building codes to see if laundry chutes are allowed in your location.

Chapter 20
Bathrooms

Obstacles are those frightful things you see when you take your eyes off your goal.

—Henry Ford

As with kitchens, remodeling a bathroom can bring a good return on investment. Homebuyers want newly updated kitchens and baths. People are building and remodeling homes to incorporate larger and nicer bathrooms, many with spa-like accouterments. As with a kitchen, space and budget will play big roles in the bathroom design. Get ideas from books, magazines, and the internet, and visit bathroom showrooms to see the latest trends in bathroom design.

If you have old cast iron bath tubs, consider resurfacing them rather than replacing them. Companies, like ARK Porcelain Refinishing, which serves the Chicagoland area, specialize in refinishing old bathtubs. Make sure the company you hire grinds out all of the old porcelain before applying a new coat. This method costs more money, but the new finish will look better and will last a lot longer. They can even spray the old bathroom wall tiles that were originally cemented in place in many older homes a new color as a cheaper alternative to the labor-intensive job of ripping out all the old tile.

It is important to note water-jet jacuzzi tubs are being replaced more and more by air-jet tubs. Water-jet tubs are known for the buildup of bacteria that accumulates in the hoses, requiring them to be cleaned frequently. Air jets do not have this problem. Whirlpool tubs come in a variety of sizes, and drains can be located in the middle or on the sides of the tub. Some whirlpool tubs have their motors in the base or in the skirt if they are built-in models; others require the motor to be mounted under the floor or a closet. A separate power outlet will be required for the motor. It is important that your architect, plumber, carpenter, and electrician all know the configuration of the tub you will purchase so they can plan accordingly.

The following pages will cover some aspects of bathroom design, including towel warmers, jacuzzi tubs, and steam showers.

Bathroom Photographs

Figure 113. The air-jet tub sits below casement windows that open to the second floor patio. Some whirlpool tubs have their motors in the base or in the skirt if they are built-in models; others require the motor to be mounted under the floor or in a closet. A motorized roller shade was installed over our tub, operated via remote control to eliminate the need to bend over the tub to pull the shade down. Click here if you are reading this on a Kindle to see the motorized shade in action: https://www.youtube.com/watch?v=d8v5XF1legs.

Figure 114. The shower is shown here before tile is laid over the dura-rock cement boards. A copper drip pan installed under the tile floor used to be standard in showers. Now, companies such as Tile Redi make precast floor pans in custom sizes. These are cemented in place over a water barrier that is applied over the subfloor. The base can then be tiled. If you want the option for a steam shower, the walls will have to be lined with a moisture barrier such as Hydro Ban and the tile filled with epoxy grout. A steam inlet pipe and conduit for the electrical controls running to the steam generator also need to be installed before the drywall and dura-rock. Depending on the unit, a steam generator can be located in a closet, under the sink, or in another remote location. A 220-volt outlet and separate drain for the steam unit will usually be required. Check the manufacturer's specs to plan for a steam shower.

Figure 115. The shower after it's been tiled. Soap dishes and shelves for shampoo and bodywash products can be built into the wall and tiled as well. Many people do not tile the shower ceiling, but the tile cuts down on moisture build-up on the ceiling and is a necessity if you plan on having a steam shower. If you want a steam shower, it is also a good idea to slope the ceiling slightly toward the wall so condensation from the steam beads toward the wall rather than dripping onto your head from the ceiling. Plan ahead for multiple shower heads, body sprays, or specialty shower heads units that might require specific roughed-in plumbing before the walls go up.

Figure 116. A large double vanity adds plenty of countertop and storage space. Be sure to seal any marble or granite countertops with a good marble sealer. I also bought a sink base large enough to accommodate a future steam generator and had the additional plumbing and electric installed under the sink.

Figure 117. The hydronic towel warmer is connected to the radiant floor heating system and serves as both a towel warmer and an additional source of heat and comfort. They also help towels dry more quickly. A thermostatic valve was installed on the towel warmer to better control the heat (valves like this can also be installed on old radiators). Electric towel warmers are available but do not provide the same level of supplemental heat for the room and only stay warm when turned on. Hydronic towel warmers only work when the home's heating system is on, but they work very well. Electric towel warmers are hardwired into a junction box behind the wall. I use a cannister-style towel warmer in the summer when the heat is off. Those work the best to envelope and warm towels.

Chapter 21
Painting and Landscaping

Hustling is putting every minute and all your effort into achieving the goal at hand. Every minute needs to count.
—Gary Vaynerchuk

Painting is the last major work that will need to be done inside. Make sure your painters take great care to cover and protect your new floors. If you do not already have a painter, get several estimates even if you are using a general contractor. We had a painting crew we had previously used several times that always did a fantastic job. Their price was also several thousand dollars below the painting estimates we received in the bids from general contractors.

Like many other items in a house, your choice of painting and decorating schemes is unlimited and will be determined by personal taste. Generally speaking, flat or matte paints are good for concealing imperfections on older or damaged walls but can be hard to clean. Flat paint is good for low-traffic areas and for ceilings. Satin or eggshell paints are great for formal areas like living and dining rooms and hallways and are easier to wipe clean. Semigloss and glossy paints deliver more shine and brighten up rooms and ceilings (Sawyers n.d.). After painting, you can add your window treatments.

If you are refinishing wood and need to strip paint, consider finding a company that will dip your doors, wood trim, and even furniture into a vat of stripping solution. It will save countless hours of stripping wood by hand with chemicals or a heat gun, which can burn the wood.

Make sure to complete all major landscaping before your new driveway and sidewalks are laid to prevent them from getting damaged or dirty. Underground sprinkler systems cost a few thousand dollars but are a great convenience. A sprinkler system should be planned out ahead of time so the needed plumbing and electrical will be available. Plant any trees, shrubs, bushes, and flowers. Once your property is free of heavy equipment, you can pour your driveway and sidewalks. Sod for new grass should be laid after the driveway and sidewalks are poured. It is time to enjoy your new home.

Bibliography

Alexander, Max. n.d. "3 Types of Flat Roofs." This Old House. Accessed December 10, 2020. www.thisoldhouse.com/roofing/21015399/3-flat-roof-types.

Allen, Keith. n.d. "How Long After a Foundation is Poured Can You Build?" Hunker. Accessed December 10, 2020. www.hunker.com/13401550/how-long-after-a-foundation-is-poured-can-you-build.

Alter, Lloyd. 2019. "Why You Shouldn't Choose Spray Foam Insulation Over Fiberglass." Treehugger. Accessed December 1, 2020. www.treehugger.com/why-you-shouldnt-choose-spray-foam-insulation-over-fiberglass-4858208.

Badore, Margaret. 2018. "Greener Alternatives to Spray Foam Insulation." Treehugger. Accessed December 1, 2020. www.treehugger.com/greener-alternatives-spray-foam-insulation-4858466.

Beall, Christine. 1991. "Installing Weep Holes." Concrete Construction. Accessed January 4, 2021. https://www.concreteconstruction.net/how-to/construction/installing-weep-holes_o.

Carter, Tim. 1995. "Cast Iron Pipes Quieter Than Plastic." *Chicago Tribune*, February 24, 1995. Accessed December 30, 2020. www.chicagotribune.com/news/ct-xpm-1995-02-24-9502240308-story.html.

———. 2003. "Ultra-low Foundation Adds to Home Flooding." *Chicago Tribune*. May 31, 2003. Accessed January 2, 2020. www.chicagotribune.com/news/ct-xpm-2003-05-31-0305310307-story.html.

Franco, Michael, and Bob Vila. n.d. "5 Things to Know Before Installing Storm Windows." Bob Vila. Accessed December 2, 2020. www.bobvila.com/articles/installing-storm-windows/.

Harvey Building Products. 2018. "6 Benefits of Installing Storm Windows." *Harveybp.com.* September 17, 2018. Accessed December 2, 2020. www.harveybp.com/blog-and-news/6-benefits-installing-storm-windows/#:~:text=Storm%20windows%20add%20insulation%20which,efficiency%20are%20the%20main%20advantages.

Heldmann, Carl. 2006. *Be Your Own House Contractor*. North Adams, MA: Storey Publishing.

Home Depot. n.d. "All About Insulation R-values." Accessed December 13, 2020. www.homedepot.com/c/ab/insulation-r-values/9ba683603be9fa5395fab9091a9131f.

Lester, Kent, and Dave McGuerty. 2016. *The Complete Guide to Contracting Your Home*, 5th ed. Blue Ash, OH: Popular Woodworking Books.

Mallach, G., M. St-Jean, M. MacNeill, D. Aubin, L. Wallace, T. Shin, K. Van Ryswyk, R. Kulka, H. You, D. Fugler, E. Lavigne, and A. J. Wheeler. 2016. "Exhaust Ventilation in Attached Garages Improves Residential Indoor Air Quality." *Indoor Air* 27 (2): 487–99. Accessed December 6, 2020. https://doi.org/10.1111/ina.12321.

Marquit, Miranda. 2020. "Home Construction Loans Explained." Bankrate. September 17, 2020. Accessed December 5, 2020. www.bankrate.com/mortgages/construction-loans-explained/.

National Trust for Historic Preservation. 2016. "Saving Windows, Saving Money: Evaluating the Energy Performance of Window Retrofit and Replacement." March 11, 2016. Accessed December 2, 2020. https://forum.savingplaces.org/connect/community-home/librarydocuments/viewdocument?DocumentKey=59eab0e4-f0f4-45c5-97c8-147a8def82ae&CommunityKey=00000000-0000-0000-0000-000000000000&tab=librarydocuments.

Palmer, Bill. 2020. "Guide to Concrete Curing Times and Methods." Concrete Network. May 8, 2020. Accessed December 10, 2020. www.concretenetwork.com/curing-concrete/.

Palmer, Bill, and Paul Newman. 2020. "Waterproofing Concrete Options for Foundations." Concrete Network. July 7, 2020. Accessed December 10, 2020. www.concretenetwork.com/concrete/waterproofing_concrete_foundations/.

Roberts, Tristan. 2011. "EPA Raises Concerns with Spray Foam Insulation." Building Green. May 16, 2011. Last updated June 1, 2018. Accessed December 1, 2020. www.buildinggreen.com/blog/epa-raises-health-concerns-spray-foam-insulation.

Roofing Calculator. 2020. "Flat Roof Materials & Installation Costs 2020." Accessed December 12, 2020. www.roofingcalc.com/flat-roof-materials/.

Sawyers, Harry. n.d. "Interior Paint Buying Guide." This Old House. Accessed December 12, 2020. https://www.thisoldhouse.com/painting/21017918/interior-paint-buying-guide.

Sisson, Patrick. "Your Old Radiator Is a Pandemic-Fighting Weapon." Bloombger.com. August 5, 2020. Accessed December 10, 2020. https://www.bloomberg.com/news/articles/2020-08-05/the-curious-history-of-steam-heat-and-pandemics.

SpacePak. n.d. Accessed December 12, 2020. www.spacepak.com/central-air-heating-and-cooling-system.

Taylor, Glenda. n.d.(a). "Solved! The Purpose of Weep Holes in Brick." Bob Vila. Accessed January 4, 2021. www.bobvila.com/articles/weep-holes-in-brick/.

———. n.d.(b). "Solved! This is How Long It Takes Concrete to Dry." Bob Vila. Accessed December 10, 2020. www.bobvila.com/articles/how-long-does-it-take-for-concrete-to-dry/.

Taylor, Glenda, and Bob Vila. "The Dos and Don'ts of Curing Concrete." Bob Vila. Accessed December 10, 2020. www.bobvila.com/articles/curing-concrete/.

Turrell, Colleen. 2000. "Storm Windows Save Energy." Home Energy. July 1, 2000. Accessed December 2, 2020. www.homeenergy.org/show/article/year/2000/id/19.

Vila, Bob. n.d. "4 Reasons Homeowners Choose Tile Roofs." Bob Vila. Accessed December 12, 2020. www.bobvila.com/articles/tile-roofs/.

Yagid, Rob. n.d. "Should Your Old Wood Windows Be Saved?" Fine Homebuilding. Accessed December 2, 2020. www.finehomebuilding.com/2010/03/11/should-your-old-wood-windows-be-saved.

Yourcarcave.com. "Do Garage Floors Have to Slope?" March 2, 2020. Accesses October 12, 2020. https://www.yourcarcave.com/do-garage-floors-have-to-slope/.

Zipkin, Nina. 2017. "50 Inspirational Quotes to Help You Achieve Your Goals." Entrepreneur. February 2, 2017. Accessed November 10, 2020. www.entrepreneur.com/article/287870.

CPSIA information can be obtained
at www.ICGtesting.com
Printed in the USA
LVHW082018200821
695769LV00013B/247